Strong Enough?

D1530013

Mark Rippetoe

ISBN 978-0-9768054-4-1

Printed in the United States of America 10 9 8 7

All essays contained herein were first published as articles in the *CrossFit Journal*. The author and publishers wish to Greg Glassman for his cooperation and encouragement in the production of this book.

Copyeditor – Carrie Klumpar
Illustration and Layout – Lon Kilgore
Project Montster – Stef Bradford

The Aasgaard Company
3118 Buchanan, Wichita Falls, TX 76308, USA
www.aasgaardco.com

Contents

"The metaphor I'm working with is this: MillBudCoors drinkers are the bench pressers of the beer world. They've lost sight of the subtlety that beer is capable of and have opted to drink a brew that does little for them besides allow them to drink a lot of it. Those who choose to go *Overhead* choose a beer that, while similar upon first glance to MillBudCoors, gives them a much fuller experience — a beer that *challenges* them."

Brock Jones on brewing a better beer

The Slow Lifts

The "slow lifts", the squat, the press, the deadlift, and the bench press, form the basis for any effective program that attempts to improve strength. And strength is very important. It is the difference between a very effective varsity athlete and a benchwarmer, an independent older person and a nursing home resident, a correctly utilized gym membership and a waste of money.

When I was a little boy, my daddy took me to work with him at his café. He worked long hours and would never have gotten to see me if I hadn't gone back to work with him in the afternoons, after his well-deserved and often interrupted nap. One of my favorite people to see at the café was the shoeshine guy from the barber shop on the corner. Roosevelt Pope was in his 50's at the time, and had social conditions differed in the early 1930's when he was young, he would have been an amazing athlete. As I remember, he was about 5'10" at probably 190 lbs., with an athletic bearing and a broad sense of humor. Roosevelt had nice big arms, but I don't know if he trained them. At the time I didn't think to ask. He brought me bubblegum from the barber shop, even though I wasn't getting a haircut, and would always tickle me a little, like loving normal adults used to be able to do to children back then.

I was always fascinated by Roosevelt's hand strength, and the things he would do to show me. He could take a stuck lid off of a jar that would embarrass my dad. He could bend a bottle cap between his thumb and his ring finger. He could do other things that I don't remember at 45 years removed, but the impression he made on me was one of confidence and power that elevated him in my esteem way above that which the unfortunate circumstances of the day would otherwise have dictated. And he was a nice man. He brought me bubblegum without even having to get a haircut.

I look back to 1961 and I see clearly that strength means way more than the ability to generate force against a resistance. It has always meant capability. It has always been the means by which people accomplished things that required them to interact with their environment. Its acquisition has always improved the acquirer in more ways than intended.

Strength is the ability to generate force against a resistance, irrespective of the movement produced by doing so. If the resistance doesn't move at all, the force exerted is still measurable with the right tools, and the muscular effort used is said to be "isometric", where the muscles stay the same length. If the movement of the resistance is controlled by something other than the muscular effort (by the exercise or measurement device) the movement is said to be "isokinetic". This is a silly thing, like a quadriceps isolation, since it does not occur in nature, or under any circumstances which the human body is designed to accommodate.

When we consider movement that is controlled by the muscular force applied to the resistance, power becomes an important concept. Power is force applied to a resistance that causes the object providing the resistance to *accelerate*, or change velocity. Force applied to a stationary force plate is a measurable quantity, but it is not power. Movement is required before power exists. In the weight room, if the weight on the bar stays the same, the faster the bar moves the more power that has been applied to it. If the weight gets lighter, it's obviously easier to move faster, so power would depend on how much faster it gets moved. As the weight decreases, power actually goes down in humans, due to the inability of a human to continue to make it go faster and faster the lighter it gets (humans have limitations inherent in the nervous system and the contractile mechanism of muscle tissue that machines don't have), and since as the weight approaches zero this limit velocity takes less and less force to acquire. Same with a heavier weight, but as the weight increases to the point where it's too heavy to lift at all, power decreases all the way to zero, since movement is required for power. At a 1RM, force is very high while power is very, very low. Powerlifting really is misnamed.

Power – the ability to accelerate – may be the most important ability to display in all sports, even those involving only the accelerated movement of the body, like gymnastics and diving. In two athletes with exactly the same skill level, the more powerful of the two will be the better athlete, since the more powerful one can utilize those skills more efficiently.

In all of sport, the highest power outputs ever measured occur during the second pull of the snatch. I would guess that the lowest would occur in the posedown at the Mr. Olympia, but I may be wrong.

Strength contributes to power by providing the force involved in the acceleration, which is obvious. Equally obvious is the fact that strength improvement will improve power, although there are other factors involved that depend on the nervous system efficiency of the individual.

Strong Enough?

Less obvious is the subtle role that strength plays indirectly in the execution of the movements dependent on power, both sports skills and power-dependent training exercises. In all expressions of power, there are elements of the kinetic chain that generate the force that produces the acceleration, and there are elements that transfer the force to the resistance.

For example, in a clean the power is generated by the extension of the knees and hips applied by the feet against the ground, and it is transferred up the back and down the arms to the bar. The efficient transfer of power along the trunk segment is possible only if the muscles that stabilize the trunk are able to hold it in perfect isometric contraction during the transfer. Any laxity in the back causes some of the power that would ideally get to the bar to be absorbed. In the same way that towing a car with a long spring is not as good an idea as using a chain, a mobile segment absorbs force that an immobile segment would transmit.

The muscles that hold the segment immobile are therefore critical to its function in the kinetic chain. A loose back during the clean produces an unfinished pull, as well as an unpredictable bar path, since varying amounts of force get to the bar. And the muscles' ability to hold an isometric contraction depend on their ability to produce sufficient force to hold all the mobile segments of the vertebral column perfectly immobile while a tremendous force is trying its best to move them.

The squat, press, deadlift, and bench press incorporate the isometric and dynamic components of the quick lifts – the snatch and the clean and jerk – because they are multijoint movements that involve lots of muscles doing lots of things during the movement. The slow lifts can all be done fast themselves, and can therefore be used to develop power as well as strength. Louie Simmons didn't invent the idea, but he taught us the lesson.

In contrast, the quick lifts cannot be done slow, and are always used to train power. They cannot be used as strength exercises, since their execution is dependent on a high bar velocity: a slow snatch will not rack; a slow clean is a deadlift. The squat can be done with heavy weights that preclude high velocities, but that *require* high force levels, and so allow force production to be trained. In novices, any movement that uses weights that are heavier than have been lifted before can produce strength increases, since they are so thoroughly unadapted to force production, and the isometric effort used in the clean and snatch will develop strength in these people. But for more advanced lifters the quick lifts are not useful for developing strength, since strength is not the limiting factor in their execution.

Of greater interest to the general public is the relationship between strength and endurance training. The media, damn near all of it, in collusion with doctors, physical therapists, athletic trainers, "exercise physiologists", high school coaches, the ACSM, the YMCA, Dr. Phil, Jake, Tony, and various other experts have all managed to equate fitness with aerobic exercise. The cruel fact is that strength training contributes mightily to endurance/aerobic training, and endurance training contributes essentially nothing to strength training.

Here's why. Let's take the example of a cyclist riding in the Hotter n' Hell Hundred, which is, after all, the largest sanctioned bicycle race in the world, right here in Wichita Falls, Texas. This cyclist, riding down the mind-numbingly flat roads of Wichita County will be able to maintain a rate of speed of about 18 mph for an agonizingly extended period of time in the sweltering August morning, unless he is killed prematurely by an inattentive oilfield worker driving onto the road, blinded by sweat and dust. This poor bastard is able to maintain his 18 mph pace by applying a uniform amount of force, x pounds, to each pedal stroke. Let's ignore that fact that he uses a complicated circular stroke, like that article in the May issue of *Bicycling* talked about, and just assume that he is pushing his pedals like most everybody does on a bicycle. Let's say that we force him to do the unthinkable and perform a correct squat in order to assess his lower body strength. After much whining about his knees and how the squat doesn't really correctly simulate the range of motion of cycling, he manages a 1RM with 135 pounds. So his pedal force constitutes a percentage of his squatting force, $x/135$. (This 1RM deal is just for the sake of illustration. I am a moral man, and I would never test a cyclist, or any other untrained squatter, at 1RM.)

Now, we blackmail him into training the squat for 8 weeks by threatening to release the pictures we took of him squatting. After an initial period of easy work to allow time for him to adapt to the unfamiliar eccentric component of the training – something absolutely necessary when training cyclists – he increases his squat from 135 x 1 to 270 x 1, a doubling of his effective leg strength.

What happens to his pedal force at 18 mph as a percentage of his max squat? It goes from $x/135$ to $x/270$: it is reduced by half. Because leg strength doubled, it now takes half of his previous force production *capacity* against the pedals to maintain the same 18 mph pace. He is stronger, and so he doesn't have to work as *hard* to do the same work.

The Slow Lifts

This analysis applies at some level to every activity that requires repeated submaximal contractions. By lowering the relative intensity of each individual effort, the cumulative effort is reduced, and depending on the range of motion of the activity, may even be shifted further toward the oxidative end of the metabolic continuum.

Although squats and all the other slow lifts are dependent upon the phosphocreatine/glycolytic energy regime, they have the ability to positively influence activities that are primarily oxidative in nature. By increasing strength and improving the efficiency of each individual component contraction, strength training makes an important contribution to every type of athletic activity.

But what about endurance training's benefit to strength training? There is no benefit to strength from aerobic training, because activities that utilize oxidative metabolism are not dependent on force production, and so do not produce a strength adaptation. Anything you can do for an uninterrupted 2 hours can't be that hard, in terms of the amount of force required. It produces endurance adaptations at the cellular level, changes that are actually detrimental to strength. Long, slow distance destroys muscle mass, beats the hell out of your knees and hips, and takes way too long.

So, you ask, why do we squat, press, deadlift? Because they work all the muscles and joints in the body, they simulate normal human movement patterns, and they produce strength appropriate to all uses for which the muscles and joints will be put. They can be trained fast or slow, done with a minimum of equipment, and form important components of the quick lifts. They affect the body in a systemic way, producing sufficient stress that a hormonal response is produced to facilitate recovery and adaptation. They are very hard. They produce psychological toughness when trained correctly. And absolutely no one has ever gotten as brutally, ungodly strong as they possibly can without doing them.

What about the bench press? The bench press is inferior to the press as an overall exercise, but it does allow for the development of greater upper-body strength than the press since the position on the bench is supported. The fact that bigger weights are done on the bench is good for upper body strength, but bad in that the limiting factor is the ability of the trunk to support the weight while it is lifted, and that doesn't get trained on the bench. So, it's a trade off. All standard commercial gyms have several benches, so do them, but be sure to use the press for at least half of your upper body work.

The squat, press, the deadlift, and the bench press have been used for decades by the strongest athletes on the planet. There is good reason for that. Any program that doesn't use them is inferior to one that does, and an athlete that leaves them out of the program is doing less than possible for performance, and less than absolutely necessary to have the best strength possible.

The Slow Lifts

"The truth is a matter of evidence, not people's feelings."

Jay P. Greene

"There's a fine line between fishing and just standing on the shore like an idiot."

Steven Wright

The Squat

The squat is the key to strength and conditioning. It is the *sine qua non* of barbell exercises. I usually go so far as to tell new trainees that if they are not going to squat, they should not even bother to train. No other exercise changes so many things about the body in so short a time as the squat. To leave them out because some uninformed fool said they were "bad for your knees" indicates that you probably didn't want to do them anyway, so it's just as well.

The next time some quasi-professional health-industry type repeats this hoary old silliness, ask them how they know. If they say that the bulk of their professional practice is generated by athletes who regularly and correctly performed full barbell squats and consequently "blew out" their knees, call me and I will be there within thirty minutes with $80 million in cash. My money is safe, of course. The truth is that the bulk of their professional practice – insofar as athletic/sports injuries are concerned (never mind the myriad injuries and conditions resulting from inactivity) – is composed of soccer, basketball, and football players with knee injuries, none of whom are ever counseled that their chosen activity will "hurt your knees." That advice is always saved for athletes participating in a structured strength program that includes squats.

I have some experience in these matters. A local pediatrician actually told one of my trainees – a particularly good kid, big and tall, but with rather limited athletic ability (he had an 8-inch vertical jump at the time) – that "I would really hate to see you jeopardize your career in athletics with a bunch of squats and weightlifting." Over the past few years this particular doctor has cost several kids a chance at an athletic scholarship and me a bunch of money, so I'm rather unhappy with him just now. And it's all the result of a profound lack of curiosity about something he desperately needs to learn.

Squats make knees stronger. Squats make athletes better. Squats are good for kids, teenagers, adults, elderly people, and anybody else who can perform them correctly. Squats are a functional expression of human skeletal and muscular anatomy, and the human body is *designed* to do them. The squat is the way that tens of millions of years of evolution has adapted the bipedal human body to lower itself to the ground. It is the position in which half the population of South Asia spends the afternoon. And when done weighted, it is the best exercise in existence for strength, power, coordination, joint integrity, bone density, confidence, discipline, intelligence, and charm.

It is important to understand why squats produce these effects. The short answer is that squats are awfully bleeding hard, and hard stuff requires more effort and produces more results than easy stuff. This is obvious to anyone who has been alive for more than five or six years.

The long answer is that since organisms adapt specifically and exactly to the stresses they are exposed to, the stresses produced by the squat happen to be the very stresses the human body needs to receive to express the genotype we have inherited. Its movement pattern is one the muscles and skeleton do anyway, the basis for bipedal locomotion and force production against the ground. When this movement is performed under progressively heavier loads, the body adapts by getting better at doing the very things it was designed to do. It adapts by increasing its ability to generate the force of muscular contraction, by coordinating those contractions more efficiently, by improving the quality of the structures that transmit the force from the ground to the load, and by getting better at doing these things exactly and specifically in accordance with the manner in which the stress is applied to the system.

To enumerate, the squat produces bigger muscles, better nervous control over those bigger muscles, denser bones, tougher tendons and ligaments, the cardiac and pulmonary capacity necessary to function under the circumstances of loaded squatting, and the psychological skills necessary to do them. Deadlifts come close, but don't quite stimulate the systemic response that deep squats produce, possibly because their range of motion is not as great, or possibly because their lack of stretch-reflex activation leaves out a key component of the stress. As of this writing these matters are poorly understood, and likely to stay that way so long as academia remains mired in the goo of dogma and conventional wisdom.

Learning to squat is not that complicated, although it can be made that way. I have developed a method over the years I have spent teaching squats to everybody who will hold still long enough, one that eliminates the usual trial-and-error approach taken by most personal trainers and strength coaches. It works well with individuals of different sizes and abilities, and with people of all ages. I have used it with deaf people, partially paralyzed people, and even stupid people, with good results. It is detailed in my and Lon Kilgore's book *Starting Strength: Basic Barbell Training*.

Strong Enough?

In a nutshell, it is easy to squat correctly if you know before you squat with the bar exactly where you are going to be when you get to the bottom. This is accomplished by assuming the desired bottom position before the bar is taken out of the rack. This way, the motor skills involved in identifying the bottom position – its balance, its proper depth, and its foot, knee, hip, back, and chest positions – can be embedded before the factor of bar load is added.

The correct stance is taken, with the heels at about shoulder width and the toes pointing out at about 30 degrees. Some people, having been told (often by a football coach) that the toes need to point straight ahead, will need to point them out more than they want to. Some people, having read the muscle magazines and seen pictures of large oily guys with no shirts and no body hair squatting with a narrow stance – "best for isolating the quads, my man" – will take a stance that is too narrow, and will need to be wider than they want to be. This stance is the best for allowing the hips to do their job of lowering and raising; it is not designed to isolate anything but rather to distribute the force evenly between the hips and knees so that everything contributes its anatomically predetermined share of the work to the job.

In this correct stance, squat down all the way to the bottom. The bottom is the extent of your full range of motion as limited by your flexibility but enabled by this correct stance. Once there, place each elbow against the inside of that knee, put the heels of the palms together, and jack your knees apart by pushing your elbows out against the inside of your knees, keeping your chest up as best you can. This puts the thighs in a position parallel with the feet, again about 30 degrees out from straight forward, with no twisting of the knee since the femur and the tibia are lined up. Your

heels will be down, since that is where they have to be if
your weight is distributed evenly on your feet. Your knees
will be slightly in front of your toes, since that is where they
will end up if your heels are down and your knees are out.
Most people will be able to get below parallel in this
position, since most of the reason people squat high is bad
position of the leg and hip components. Squatting below
parallel is perfectly natural if the correct position is used. If it
weren't, it wouldn't be so easy to do.

Once this position is comfortable and stretched out a
little, come up out of the bottom position and pay attention
to what you do on the way up. Ninety percent of people
who have had no previous instruction in the squat will lead
up out of the bottom with their hips, essentially shoving
their butt up in the air. This is correct. The squat is a hips-
initiated movement, meaning that hip extension – glutes,
hamstrings, and adductors acting to return the pelvis/low
back and the femurs to a straight line – starts the squat up out
of the hole.

The trick is to keep the chest up while this happens.
Keeping the chest up and *lifting* the chest are two different
things. "Keeping the chest up" involves maintaining the angle
and position of the back while hip drive occurs, while "lifting
the chest" involves changing that angle and position.
Attempting to increase the angle of the back (by actually
lifting the chest) while coming out of the hole will pull you
forward, off your heels on to your toes, and kill your hip
drive, in addition to exposing your spine to changing
leverages under load as its angle increases. The back will
become vertical when it is supposed to at the end of the
movement, without you doing anything other than returning

to a fully erect position. Making the back vertical too early, or trying to keep it too vertical in the bottom, interferes with the mission of the hips.

Here's a test that can be very illustrative of the concept of hip drive and its relationship to these angles. Take your correct bottom position and then have a training partner put a hand on your lower back, applying force straight down, perpendicular to the floor, as gravity would do. Drive up against this force while keeping your back angle constant, and see what this feels like. Now do the same thing while raising your chest up and increasing your back angle. I predict that you will not like it as well.

While we're at it, compare driving up against the hand while looking down at a point six to ten feet ahead on the floor, to driving up while looking up at the ceiling. I predict that you will like looking down much better. This is because looking up pulls up your chest and shifts your weight forward onto your toes, while looking down at that angle puts the cervical spine in an anatomically normal position. Looking down also allows the eyes to provide the brain with instantaneous information regarding body position relative to a stationary point close enough to serve as a balance reference.

So, here's the bottom line: your hips cannot drive up if your weight is balanced forward on your toes, and if your heels are not planted firmly, your weight is forward. This is because of the way the hamstrings work during the squat: they pull back against their insertion points on the tibia just below the knee, producing a stretch-reflex-enhanced contraction up out of the bottom. The tibia should be a solid anchor for this "bounce." The hamstrings use their *proximal* function in the squat – they pull on the ischial tuberosity of the pelvis to produce hip extension – the straightening out of the hip. No forward knee travel should occur after the hamstrings begin to tighten as the bottom of the squat is approached or as the upward drive occurs, since any forward knee movement (which can be thought of as backward movement of the distal end of the tibia relative to the knee) will diminish hamstring tension and make the stretch-reflex-enhanced hamstring contraction much less powerful. If the heels are not planted firmly, some of the force generated against the tibia gets absorbed as the heel gets pushed down, instead of pulling the pelvis into extension. In the squat, the tibia is the anchor for the hamstrings, and it can't anchor anything if its distal end at the heel is squishy.

All these things can be best studied and worked out before the bar is on the back. Most of the problems encountered in the squat can be fixed here, without load. Only after a good position is obtained at the bottom without weight should you squat with the bar. Fortunately, most people need only a couple of minutes in the position before they're ready to use the bar.

When you're ready, take the bar out of the rack (stepping back please, so that you walk forward when putting it up), take the same stance you prepared, look down a bit, think about keeping your knees out, take a big breath and hold it, and squat all the way down. I'd bet a lot of money – maybe not $80 million, but a lot – that this first squat is balanced, strong, deep, and correct.

There is a lot here to consider, and this is just the beginning. It is the most important barbell exercise in our inventory of things to do in the gym. Learn to do it correctly, dammit. We need you strong.

"I can win an argument on any topic, against any opponent. People know this, and steer clear of me at parties. Often, as a sign of their great respect, they don't even invite me."

Dave Barry

The Press

The press is the oldest barbell exercise in the gym. As with many old things, its value often goes underappreciated.

Picking up a weight and pushing it overhead is so basic a movement that one suspects some sort of DNA-type explanation for it. Children can be observed doing this to show off for their buddies. Pre-literate civilizations in Borneo probably have a name for picking up logs from endangered rain forest trees and then putting them overhead, completely unaware of the threat this poses to the Planet. Quite literally, the first thing that was ever done with a barbell was a standing press, because it is the logical thing to do with a barbell, once you have picked it up.

Fifty years ago, if a fellow physical culturist wanted to know how strong you were, the question would have been, "How much can you press?" It was reckoned that a man should have been able to press his bodyweight. Since not many women (Abbye "Pudgy" Stockton being a very important and gorgeous exception) had at that time figured out they weren't going to get big ol' ugly muscles from lifting weights, these ancient people would probably not have known that a woman should be able to press 2/3 of her bodyweight. Of course these numbers can only apply to people who actually train the lift. Most people don't. They bench press instead.

I am a cynical bastard. I truly believe that the reason typical commercial gym members would rather bench press is because they get to lay down. (Not that the bench press is useless; we will investigate its usefulness in detail later.) Same thing with leg presses, leg extensions, leg curls, lying triceps extensions, seated anythings, preacher anythings, and Pilates. If you're trying to relax after a strenuous day in the cubicle, go ahead and do your yoga class, finish up with some seated alternate 3 lb. dumbbell presses on a balance ball, and have yourself a nice smoothie. But if you want to get strong, it's probably going to involve standing with a heavy bar in your hands.

First, let's get some nomenclature problems out of the way. In resistance exercise, the general term "press" refers to a multi-joint extension that drives an external resistance away from the body. (In gymnastics, the term refers to movements that use the body itself as resistance.) So the squat is not a press – the bar is not being driven away; the bar loads the trunk segment which is then lowered and raised – the leg press is actually a press (it used to be done with a bar balanced on the feet while lying on the ground under it, until someone realized how incredibly stupid this was). If we use the term "press" specifically in reference to barbell exercise, we mean a standing overhead press with a bar in both hands, the older term for this being the "two-hands press" which has been shortened over the years to the simpler form. Anything that modifies this movement must be described with a qualifying term. The Military Press is a press done in strict "military fashion", with heels together and no torso movement, sometimes with the back against a wall. (Things have gone so far down the toilet with respect to weight room terminology that the typical Gold's Gym personal trainer thinks a Seated Behind-the-Neck press is a military press.) A Dumbbell Press is a standing press done with a dumbbell in each hand simultaneously unless the alternating version, or the one-handed version is specified. A Push Press is done with the help of the legs and hips, which start the upward momentum of the bar and can add as much as 30% to the weight that can be used.

Pressing a bar overhead develops core strength, and somehow manages to do this without a Swiss Ball. Since the kinetic chain – the parts of the body involved in the transmission of force from the places where it is generated to the places where it is applied – in the press starts at the ground and ends at the hands, everything in between these two points gets worked, one way or another. This pretty much includes everything. Specifically, the trunk and hip muscles have to stabilize the body while the force being generated by the arms and shoulders gets transmitted between the bar and the floor. This can get really hard when the weight gets up close to 1RM, and heavy presses require and develop a thick set of abs and obliques. Vasily Alexeyev – the "Big Russian" weightlifter from the 1970s, and the strongest presser in history – was not merely a fat man.

In contrast, the kinetic chain in the bench press extends from the bench, or more correctly from the place where the back and the bench connect, to the bar. Good benchers brace against the ground with the legs, but the exercise still omits the active balancing and stabilizing work that the core must do in a standing press.

Working toward a bodyweight press is a laudable goal. It provides an appreciation of, and a connection with, an important part of the history of weight training, a time when equipment was simple and training was straightforward. When you press, you train with Kono, Alexeyev, Starr, Grimek, and Cyr. When you press, you train much more than the shoulders and arms. You train the soul of the sport of barbell exercise.

The press we will perform will not be a strict military press, but it will be stricter than an old-style Olympic weightlifting press. It starts at the rack or the squat stands with an empty bar, set at about the same height as a squat, at the middle of the sternum. The grip will be just outside the shoulders, wide enough that the index fingers clear the deltoids, not so wide that the arms drive out at an angle on the way up. For most people this will be between 18 and 22 inches. The thumbs should be around the bar and the heel of the palm should be as close as possible to the bar, well down away from the fingers so that it is close to the bones of the forearm that will drive it up.

Take the EMPTY bar out of the rack and step back one step. The bar should rest on your shoulders with your elbows in front of the bar. This is an important detail, since if the elbows are behind the bar, you will drive it away from you on the way up. Your flexibility may not permit a good position at first, and the bar may not want to sit down on your shoulders properly, but flexibility will come with time and a proper press can be done as long as the elbows are in front of the bar.

Your stance will be comfortable and wide, wider than a pulling stance and maybe almost as wide as a squat stance. A strict military press is supposed to be harder, and a very close stance certainly makes it that way. Our object is to see how strong we can get using the press, and stability should not be a concern.

Look straight ahead to a point on the wall level with your eyes, and lift your chest. This is accomplished with the muscles of the upper back, and can be thought of as raising your sternum up to your chin. This fixes several position problems that usually result in a bad bar path, and improves tightness in the upper torso between reps.

Take a big breath, hold it, and drive the bar up over your head. (Hold your breath while the bar is moving. This increased pressure provides support for the back and chest, and is essential for safety when moving heavy weights. This is discussed at length in my and Lon Kilgore's book *Starting Strength: Basic Barbell Training*). In the lockout position, most people will leave the bar slightly in front of the head at first, so make sure that the bar is back far enough that it lines up over the shoulder blades and the middle of the foot – that a vertical line from the bar down to the mid-foot intersects the scapulas. This is where the bar must be if it is to be locked out in balance. Once there, the elbows should be locked and the shoulders shrugged up so that the bar is supported by the skeletal components and the traps, and not just the triceps. This is the position the bar is going to be at the end of every correct rep.

From your correct starting position, lean back very slightly and drive the bar up as close as possible to your face. As soon as the bar passes the top of your head, get under the bar. Move your body forward under the bar and use this motion to help lock the bar out at the top. Don't move the bar back, move *your body* forward. When this is done correctly, the forward movement of the body helps straighten out the shoulder, which helps drive up the elbow into lockout.

There will be a small amount of movement involved in getting the bar from a position in front of the neck to a point over the shoulder blades. This distance should be made up with the forward movement of the body, not the backward movement of the bar. Pushing the bar back instead of up is inefficient and misses the opportunity to leverage the elbows into extension with the powerful hip extensors working through a properly rigid torso. Abdominal, low back, and hip strength – "core" stability – make this possible, and make pressing an incredibly effective core exercise.

Start with the empty bar and do a set of five. Add a little weight, 20 or 30 lbs. if you're as huge, massive, and powerful as I am, 10 or even less if you're intelligent enough to appreciate the usefulness of maintaining good form while learning a new movement, and go up doing sets of 5 until the bar speed starts to slow. Stay there and do two more sets, and call it a workout.

The press is hard. You won't be able to press what you can bench. You have to support with your whole body what the bench supports when you lay down to press. So you're doing all the work instead of letting the bench do some of it, supporting, balancing, and manhandling the whole load. This is how strength was, and is, built.

That's Dr. Craig Whitehead in the
blue checkered shirt, Qviniek
& Bill March.
You should recognize Sup.
Makes me glad I do my
sit-ups.

"Passive acceptance of the teacher's wisdom is easy to most boys and girls. It involves no effort of independent thought, and seems rational because the teacher knows more than his pupils; it is moreover the way to win the favour of the teacher unless he is a very exceptional man. Yet the habit of passive acceptance is a disastrous one in later life."

Bertrand Russell

The Deadlift

I know of no better example of functional strength than a 600-pound deadlift. Except a 700-pound deadlift. That's what strength is: the ability to generate force, and the "functional" part is really just a qualifier. Because when you're that strong, it's functional. That's the part that has the modern "academic" wing of the fitness industry in such a fog just now.

It is currently fashionable to characterize certain types of training as "functional" and other types of training as something else, maybe "non-functional" or "training that lacks function" or "functionless" training. I have no idea why this has received such attention recently, except that there are several equipment manufacturers that make stuff that is supposed to add "function" to our training. And damned if it doesn't always involve some sort of instability that the overcoming of provides the primary benefit.

But more than involving instability (and expensive proprietary devices), it also always seems to involve very light weights. Look, if a guy wants to do his alternate dumbbell presses while seated on a stability ball, that's fine with me. But my god, you *have* to use more than the 15-pound dumbbells! Because if you want functional strength, you have to at some point get strong enough to lift more than the 15s. You just *do*. But this point often gets lost on stability ball day.

And I swear that I actually saw a guy doing 50-pound behind-the-neck lat pulldowns *while seated on a Swiss ball*. I was out of town, by the way, in a state that begins with a C.

Strong Enough?

It seems as though whenever we talk about functional strength, we get all hung up on the functional part and forget about the *strength* part. So I'm going to go out on a limb here and suggest something that may upset the PTs and the ATCs and the exercise physiologists that seem to be so fond of this stuff. My contention is that if you make your deadlift go from 185 up to 400, you have obtained functional strength without the use of anything but a weighted barbell. Furthermore, if you do this, your seated alternate dumbbell stability ball press will go up too, without having to suffer the embarrassment of actually doing it in public.

The deadlift teaches function, because there is no more functional a movement than picking up something heavy. It's one of the things our bodies are built to do, and when we do it as an exercise, we get better at using our bodies the way they were built to be used. We just need to make sure we're doing it right, since when we learn it right as an exercise, it carries over into all the other situations where "functional" is important.

I had a little business venture a couple years ago that was going to make me and Carla, my associate here at Wichita Falls Athletic Club, millions of dollars in a short time. *Fistfuls* of cash, I tell you. Why, had it worked I wouldn't be writing this now, because there would just not be enough time. We were going to teach the deadlift to industrial and commercial employees, for the purpose of applying the skill to workplace situations and thus preventing back injuries. The idea was sound, I'm still convinced, but it was not something the corporate human resources people were willing to give up the paper clip money for. We eventually got tired of trying to sell the idea to people who had no idea how a reduction in the incidence of $500,000 back injuries could save them money. I'm actually glad we got it out of our systems, before we got our faces sued off by a plaintiff's attorney representing some fat guy with a back injury he got in his garage.

The deadlift has the reputation of being even more hated than the squat. Even people who will actually do their squats will sneak out of the gym before I notice that they haven't gotten the bar down on the floor. This disappoints me, but I understand it. Deadlifts are hard. Most people don't like hard stuff. That's why there are more people doing one-arm triceps kickbacks on the wobble board with the 5-pounders than there are people doing deadlifts. And the deadlift is hard to cheat; a squat can be high and people might disagree, but a deadlift is easy to judge.

It is actually a very simple exercise, requiring only a couple of important technical considerations and a willingness to pull on things that would rather not move. The two technical considerations are back position and the bar path.

The lower back needs to be extended, or arched, during the entire pull so the bones of the spine stay in the right position to bear a load safely. The thoracic spine needs to be in a correct position too, best accomplished by keeping the chest up during the pull. The position is the same one that you assume when standing erect normally and correctly, referred to as "normal anatomical position." The low back arch is not natural for some people, and it must be worked on and coached diligently if it is not right. The upper back, "chest-up" position can cause problems with our other main consideration, the bar path, if it is not understood clearly.

Strong Enough?

When the bar gets heavy, the bar path of a correct deadlift will be essentially vertical. This is because the straight line of a vertical pull is the shortest distance between the floor and lockout, and this is the way your body likes to do heavy deadlifts. Don't lose your balance and fall (this is the stability part). There will be an angle, defined by the plane of the flat back as it intersects the floor, which produces the most efficient pull off the floor. That angle will allow the best use of the quads as they straighten the knees for the initial push, it will allow the bar to stay on the shins as it comes vertically up, and it will keep the bar in contact with the legs until it locks out at the top. This back angle will be maintained as the knees straighten out and the bar passes them on the way up, until the hips begin to extend and the knees and hips lock out together.

If the back angle is too horizontal – too parallel to the floor – the net effect is the removal of the quads from the pull. Quads straighten out the knee. That is their anatomical function, but it must occur while the bar is moving up, not before, or the muscle group has not contributed to the pull. Think of it this way: in a good deadlift, the knees push the bar away from the floor, and the hips pull it to lockout. If the knees start out straight (or straighten before the bar rises above them), you have done a stiff-leg deadlift, an assistance exercise for the hamstrings.

If the back angle is too vertical, the hips will rise before the bar leaves the floor, straightening out the knee without moving the bar up, and pulling the shins back away from the bar so that there is air between bar and shin. This wastes movement, but, more important, it puts the bar in a bad mechanical position to pull, too far away from the hips – the point of rotation around which the force of leg drive is turning. Then the bar either stays too far away from the legs during the pull or it bangs you in the shins as it comes back in line where it should have been. Either way, the pull is inefficient and incorrect.

Furthermore, the most efficient angle will be a little different for everybody, since it depends on individual anthropometry – the differences in the lengths of the segments of the body: the arms, the spine, the femurs, and the tibias. People with long torsos and short legs will have a steeper back angle than people with long legs and short torsos. At the correct back angle, the only things that are constant are the bar in contact with the shins, the shoulders very slightly in front of the bar, and the back locked into normal anatomical position. If you're coaching, don't expect there to be a template that everybody fits. Right is relative.

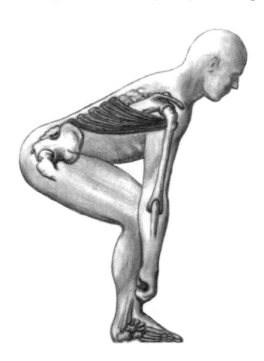

These effects are observed mainly when the bar gets heavy. At light weights all manner of mistakes are possible because the bar path can be a crooked line and the universe does not care. However, what with gravity being the law, at heavy weights the bar path will be damned close to vertical, possibly with a very slight arc back toward the legs as it comes off the floor, and you will have to learn to like it and adapt accordingly.

Now, the chest position has an effect on the starting position (sorry if this is getting dry, we're almost through with the concentration part) due to the fact that many people confuse chest-up with back angle. Lifting the chest is a thoracic spine extension, done with the muscles of the upper back. When you lift the chest, you do it by straightening out the curve between the T1 and T8 vertebrae, tightening the upper slips of the longissimus dorsi, and producing an isometric contraction that holds the vertebrae immobile during the deadlift. Theoretically, at least. The whole spine should be protected by this isometric contraction. In effect, the hips and legs generate the movement – they are the motor. The locked back transfers this movement down the arms to the bar – it is the transmission.

This must be understood: the chest-up position has nothing to do with the back angle. The chest can be lifted by the thoracic contraction in any position, standing straight up or bent over at the waist. So can the lower back extension, the movement that tightens the muscles that protect the lumbar spine. This skill needs to be developed so that a tight back position can be assumed whenever it is necessary, in any position, whether deadlifting or picking up the groceries, skiing really fast downhill or staying tight while you hit the nose guard, maintaining a tight torso during a sprint or carrying a charged hose up the third flight of stairs.

This is precisely why the deadlift is as functional as exercise gets. Name a physical movement that applies in more situations or that occurs as frequently as generating force against the ground and transferring it to a load in the hands. Nothing that involves a big yellow ball gets even close.

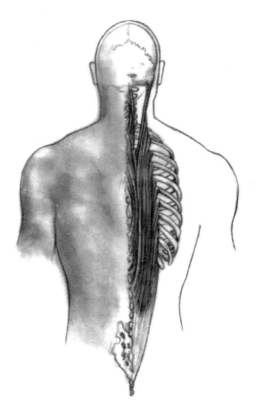

The erector spinae.

Strong Enough?

The Bench Press

The longer I stay in this business, the less fond I become of the bench press. And it's not the fault of the exercise itself, which is a perfectly reasonable thing to do if it's incorporated correctly into the program.

It's the injured shoulders, the big pecs and little legs, the $400, six-layer denim/moly-steel shirts, the 18-year-old football players who can "do 500," the spotters with traps more fatigued than the bencher's pecs.

But mainly, it's the noise.

Not at my gym, of course. The vast majority of my members learned a while back that the best way to keep their shoulders healthy was to press and bench press in equal doses, quietly. But there are other gyms in which the bench press is the only upper-body lift done and is the main trapezius exercise for spotters, since deadlifting is pretty scarce in these places. And the yelling just annoys my ass all out of proportion to how much it should. I get really tired of spotters trying to sound like Macho Man Randy Savage, with their hands on the bar "spotting" every rep. At WFAC, spotters don't touch the bar unless it's going back down or has been stuck for long enough to get them worried. We all squat and pull, so our legs are generally in proportion. Just now there are no competitive powerlifters here, so most of the members don't even know what a bench shirt is. (Quite honestly, if a bunch of them starting spending money on bench shirts, I'd probably feel compelled to raise my dues.) Here, benching is just another exercise, not the absolute measure of personal worth it is in some circles, and the noise level is commensurate with this more balanced, peaceful, logical worldview.

The bench press is the best exercise for absolute strength in the upper body, because it allows the lifter to move heavier weights with the arms than any other exercise. It should be included in every barbell training program. But it is not the only lift we should do, and it frequently gets used as though it is.

Benching provides hard active work for the chest, shoulders, and arms and isometric work for the forearms, and it trains novice lifters well in the fundamental skill of pushing on a very heavy load. This last may be its most useful function. When people first start training, they have no experience with maximal effort. The vast majority of humans on this planet have never had to push really, really hard on anything, and that is a skill that should be developed, along with cooking, critical thinking, and interpersonal relations. The bench press is a very good place to learn how to bear down and push hard, and this invaluable lesson translates to all the other slow lifts quite well.

This is because the bench press is relatively simple to do and, once learned correctly, involves not much more than this: pushing very hard on something that is moving rather slowly because it is very damned heavy.

There are no other distractions since the back is braced against the bench, and the rest of the body – while it must be controlled in terms of position and tension – is not directly involved in the lift. Pushing hard is possible because the segment doing the pushing is very short, and the thing – or one of the things – you are pushing against, the bench, does not move at all. (Yes, you push against the bench too. The bench and the bar are pushed apart.) The press involves the entire body down to the floor, and while this makes it a better exercise overall, it also means that some extraneous movement will occur in the supporting segment secondary to the prime movers used in the exercise. The bench press allows you to focus on the "push" itself, without having to worry about controlling much of the rest of the body at the same time. This allows you to bench press more weight than you can press.

The two exercises thus provide balance in a couple of ways: the bench press works the anterior shoulder girdle and chest, while the press works the medial and posterior shoulder, and the posterior stabilizers. The bench press works on raw "push" while the press trains total body stability while pushing. Both are best done without a lot of unnecessary drama.

Since everybody pretty much knows how to bench press, at least in general terms, I'll address just a couple of points I consider salient. First, there is a little trick I use to make the bar go to the right place, through the right path, every time. It involves eye position, and it applies to every sport that involves the use of an implement, from benching to golf to tennis to throwing the shot. (Many other coaches have observed this, and I just stole from them. I am shameless in this way.) When you take the bar out of the rack, you'll be looking up, since you're lying on your back. Find a place on the ceiling to stare at and nail your eyes to that place. This point will be your positional reference for the bar path and its lockout position over the chest. If you return the bar to the same position against the ceiling at the top of every rep, having touched the same place on your chest every time, you will find that your bar path is uniform as well. This is due to the use of the stationary reference for the movement – the fixed point on the ceiling.

In golf, you look at the ball, not the club head. The head of the club goes to where the eyes are fixed. You look at the ball in a tennis volley, and, even though the ball is moving, your head moves with it and renders it stationary relative to your eyes. The implement in your hand then goes where it is directed by the eyes: the racket goes to the ball, the shot goes downfield, and the bar in your hands will go to the same place in reference to the ceiling if you fix your eyes on that point. Most bench pressers do this without thinking about it. It has been my observation that very few good benchers look at the bar as it moves, since it is liable to move to a different place each time if the eyes follow the bar instead of directing it to the *right* place.

Use this technique next time you teach someone how to bench and see what happens. More than 90% of the time, their first reps will be almost perfect if the movement is explained this way.

But how, you ask, does this observation relate to, for instance, the snatch? Damn you, you're making me have to think. Okay, the snatch is a movement that involves the bar moving from the ground to overhead, and would be impossible to watch against the ceiling due to the neck position this would require. More importantly, a movement like the snatch or the clean is best thought of as a movement of the body, not the bar. As such, we normally fix the gaze on the facing wall, so that positional reference information is available about the body itself, not the bar, which will go to the right place if the body does its job correctly. As a general rule, there must be some fixed reference point for the eyes in any kind of movement of the body, and in every barbell (or dumbbell) exercise that fixed point should be stationary.

Next, the bench press, as mentioned before, has a little bitty short kinetic chain that goes from the hands to the place where the back contacts the bench. It would be better if we could involve more of the body in the movement, and as it turns out good benchers know how to do this. They brace against the floor with their feet, pushing the chest up and arching the back, in effect extending the kinetic chain on down to the floor. It is very common to see novice benchers raise one foot up in the air as they miss a heavy rep. I have no idea why this is so universal a reflex, but it is so normal to do this that I caution my other members to stay away from the new people's feet when they do their work sets the first few times. Obviously, if a foot comes up, a less-than-efficient use of the legs has occurred. The best foot position is open to discussion, but I like to use a stance that is about like the squat stance, with feet about shoulder width apart and shins approximately vertical. This produces the best drive down the bench with less tendency to bridge the butt up, as might be the case if the feet were too far back up under the hips.

Now, it is bad form to raise the butt up off the bench, and what *should* happen is that the push from the legs is directed straight along the bench to the back and shoulders instead of up so that the arch is supported without a loss of contact with the bench at the hips. This convention is designed to prevent things from getting too out of hand, turning the bench press into a decline bench press, an easier version of the exercise with a shorter range of motion. Our purpose is to get strong using the bench press, not to see how much weight we can bench press, which is an entirely different matter. So we need to keep our butts on the bench while using our legs to support our position.

Some people prefer to bench press with their feet up on the bench, or even held up in the air. This is fine, as long as everybody is aware of what is being compromised when this is done. A lower back injury or a preference for a harder style might make this desirable, but it is less efficient, and not as much weight can be lifted this way. But, remembering that more weight is not always the point, use this if you want or need to.

Dumbbell bench presses are a very good substitute for the barbell version. The DB bench is actually the older of the two exercises, dumbbells having been pressed in the supine position on a bench before the invention of the upright support bench that allowed the barbell version of the lift to be performed without spotters. Prior to the invention of that equipment, the lifter would have to clean the bar, lie down with it, press it, stand up with it, and then set it down on the floor (which didn't leave much gas for that 500-pound set of five that all the high school powerlifters seem to be able to do today). The DB bench involves more of the body, and quite a bit of skill when using heavy dumbbells if the shoulders are not to be dislocated.

The bench press is an important exercise that has suffered at the hands of people who lack the proper perspective of its value, its correct use, and its limitations. Use it wisely.

And tell your spotters to be quiet. Please.

Working with a client in the 80's. The origins of the Starting Strength teaching method.

Strong Enough?

"Perhaps the most valuable result of all education is the ability to make yourself do the thing you have to do, when it ought to be done, whether you like it or not; it is the first lesson that ought to be learned; and however early a man's training begins, it is probably the last lesson that he learns thoroughly."

Thomas H. Huxley

The Power Clean

When I first started lifting seriously, I had the good fortune to meet Bill Starr in the weight room at what was then Midwestern University in Wichita Falls, Texas. I was a snotty-nosed little smartass at the time and despite the fact that I knew absolutely nothing then about either training or being an effective smartass, I presumed that I did. Bill taught me about both.

I had been training – or, rather, working out – with a guy on faculty at the school, not getting much accomplished. We were doing half-squats. There, I said it, and I'm happy to get it off my chest. In my defense, I didn't know any better, and the other guy, who should have, didn't either. Novices left to their own devices in the weight room will usually decide to do things the easy way, and then come up with an explanation that makes perfect sense to other novices.

I was "training" by myself one afternoon in the dead of summer in 1979 when I ran into Bill in the weight room. He was in town dealing with family in the aftermath of our famous tornado of April 10 that year. Things were still rather hectic, and I had run in for a workout at what was not my normal time. I saw the unfamiliar face on my way in, and wondered who the long-haired guy was (the Falls is a smaller town than its population would indicate). I began the workout with my cute little partial squats and had gotten up to 225 when he asked me, while I was still under the bar, "Just what in the hell are those things you're doing there?" I tried to explain to the new guy what a squat was, and over the course of the next few minutes became aware of the fact that this was not a "new guy."

43

Now, Bill is not one to beat you over the head with advice. He has never been nearly as concerned with being listened to as I used to be. I have learned over the years why he is not. How is it in my best interest for an 18-year-old kid, or for that matter a 45-year-old football coach, to believe me when I say that squats should be done below parallel? Or that presses are a better exercise for sports than bench presses? Or why snatches are important for powerlifters? I guess that at some level it is important just to *be right*, but the older I get, the less important it becomes to me that everyone else recognize that I am. Bill knows what he knows, and he offered to help me, if I would listen. But his feelings were not hurt when I was stubborn. He was past all that. I am trying to get that way.

Bill worked with me for several years while he was here. He was in town more often then. I value the things he taught me. One of those things was to try to be more receptive to instruction. One day while we were benching at David Anderson's gym he tried to explain some fine point of technique that had eluded me, and for some reason I wasn't trying very hard to learn. He stepped back and said, "You know, it would be better if you would get more coachable." I thought about that a lot, and I have tried to get and stay more coachable. This requires that I be mindful of the fact that I have many things to learn, even – maybe especially – about things I think I already know.

Those of us who worked with Billy all learned the power versions of the Olympic lifts, even if we were powerlifters. Among those, of course, was the power clean. It took me just one workout to get pretty good at it. He was a good teacher. We didn't do the squat clean, and I didn't ask why, since I actually didn't know what it was until later. Power cleans worked just fine for what we needed: learning to apply power in the pull, for purposes of improving our deadlifts. He deals with them in his famous book *The Strongest Shall Survive*.

I have now been coaching the Olympic lifts for almost twenty years and am well aware that the full squat clean is a very important movement, both for motor skill development and for full-body conditioning. Learning it is important, since it is complicated, and learning complicated things improves the ability to learn. But I still teach the power clean to my novices first, just like Bill did. This is not because I can't teach the squat clean to inexperienced lifters. I can, and I have. But I choose not to because I think it interferes with learning the squat correctly.

The front squat – the "squat" part of the squat clean – and the back squat are two very different movements that happen to be similar enough to cause problems for a novice lifter. The back squat depends on hip drive for power out of the bottom, and relies on an initial hip extension. This is accomplished by reaching back with the hips, which places the back at an angle quite a bit forward of the vertical. The form I teach places the bar on the back, below the traps, right below the spine of the scapula, allowing the hips to be driven straight up out of the bottom very efficiently if the back is at the proper angle. The bar/squatter system is in balance with a heavy weight when the bar is over the middle of the foot, and for most people this happens when the hips are back, the knees are just in front of the toes, and the back is at about 45 degrees. I don't like the traditional high-bar, or Olympic, back squat specifically because the longer lever arm produced by the higher bar position and the resulting higher torque on the lower back reduces the efficiency of the hip drive.

The front squat depends on a nearly vertical back angle, since the bar is carried on the front of the shoulders. The most efficient back angle is as nearly vertical as possible, since any forward lean increases rotational torque against the lower back and predisposes the lifter to drop the bar. The cue for the front squat is "chest up" or "elbows up," which makes the back stay vertical. The bar in a back squat is wedged in between the back and the hands, and is much harder to drop; a front squat is so easy to drop that spotting the movement is both unnecessary and dangerous. The bar still gets driven up out of the bottom with a hip extension, since that's what has to happen to stand up, but this occurs without the benefit of the hamstrings; they are in a shortened position due to the back angle and the knee angle, and cannot contract since they are *already contracted* in this position. The front squat therefore depends primarily on the glutes for hip extension. Hips are easier to drive up when they are back away from the heels and the hamstrings are in an extended position to help with active hip extension, and this is why the back squat allows the use of much heavier weights, at least when it is done correctly.

The full squat style does indeed make the clean easier to rack, since the act of dropping under the bar to receive it with a front squat produces a faster elbow rotation. But for a novice trainee who is not an Olympic lifting prospect, I am more interested in a correct back squat than a fast rack in the clean. I can fix slow elbows later, but I want the back squat to be right from the beginning because I am more interested in strength for novices. The front squat and the back squat are very different movements, true, but not to a novice: to a person unfamiliar with either one, they are both just squatting down very low with the bar. If the full squat clean is taught along with the back squat the first couple of weeks, the vast majority of novice lifters end up doing a back squat with a vertical back, knees way out over the toes and no hip drive. If you decide to teach the squat clean, it is much better, I think, to wait a month until the back squat is automatic, so that the front squat part of the squat clean can be kept separate in the lifter's motor mind.

In fact, I'll go out on a limb here and say that Olympic lifters should probably learn to back squat with a low bar position, since it allows the use of heavier weights, and it is the only exercise in the weight room that specifically trains hip drive. After all, why do Olympic lifters do the back squat? It is not a contested lift. The front squat is another exercise anyway. The high back angle of the Olympic squat is not reproduced in the pull of either the snatch or the clean. In fact, weightlifting coaches advise their athletes to keep the back angle as high as possible in their back squats precisely to reduce the low back torque that the long lever arm produces, and this angle ends up being more vertical than that used on either of the pulls. It's like trying to make the back squat into a slightly different version of the front squat. But that misses the point of the back squat. Olympic lifters squat to get their hips, legs, trunk, and back strong, like everybody else does. Since the low bar position allows the use of heavier weights in a position more similar to that of the pulls, and works the low back at an angle more useful for the pull, I submit that it is better for weightlifters, and everyone, to do it this way.

While I'm at it, deadlifts would be good for weightlifters too. Some critics have argued that heavy deadlifts slow the clean pull off the floor. It seems to me, though, that if the deadlift is trained enough to get it up to about 150% of the clean, it would *speed up* the clean pull off the floor quite a bit. Weightlifting does involve strength after all, at least at the international level. But – I'll say it for you – what the hell does Rippetoe know?

Excuse the digression. We were talking about the power clean.

The power clean teaches explosion. It cannot be done slowly. And since it involves a longer pull than the squat clean, it emphasizes the finish, where the maximum hip, knee, and ankle extension occurs, without the added complication of the front squat part of the movement. The reason that the clean is so critical to sports performance training is that it is a scalable way to develop power. There will be a weight, however light or heavy, that the athlete can use correctly for the clean. That weight can be gradually added to, enabling athletes of any level of advancement to increase power production. Since athletics depends so heavily on the ability to exert force rapidly, the clean is a very useful tool for all athletes. I like power cleans better, for the reasons discussed above, and because none of the power production aspects of the clean are particular to the full squat version. The top part of the pull is where power is at maximum anyway, and the power clean emphasizes this over the squat clean because the bar has to be pulled higher – and therefore harder – to rack it.

The power clean is best thought of as a jump with the bar in the hands, followed immediately by an upward forward slam of the elbows to rack it on the shoulders. It is much easier to learn from the hang position; learning it off the floor tends to understate the importance of the explosive phase at the top. In fact, the reason the power clean is an important assistance exercise for weightlifters is that it teaches the "finish" of the pull at the top, that last little bit of extension that must be done before going under the bar. If the first thing learned is the jump, the trainee has a better chance of keeping the power part of the movement foremost in importance.

The most important position is what I refer to as the "jumping" position. It is the point at which the bar touches the thigh when both the hips and knees are unlocked and the arms are still straight. It is the point at which Olympic lifters start what they call the second pull. If the bar touches this point every time the clean is pulled, the back will be vertical enough that the jump, and the bar, will go straight up without going forward. If the clean is first learned from this point, with a jump and a slam of the elbows, it is easy to gradually lower it down the legs to the floor, reinforcing the jumping position each time the bar slides back up the legs.

There are just a few important things to keep in mind. First, the bar always leaves the thighs on the way up from the jumping position. This means that the bar will be touching (but not crashing into) the thighs at that point, and as a result is not out away from the body when the jump starts. Second, the elbows are kept straight until *after* the jump begins. Pulling with bent elbows is a terribly common, unproductive habit that causes some of the pulling force to be absorbed in the straightening-out of the bent elbow. This results in highly variable pulling efficiencies, with differing amounts of force being transferred to the bar. Likewise, the third important thing to remember is that the back must be held flat, as rigid and tight as possible so that efficient, predictable, reproducible force transmission between the hips/legs and the bar takes place. The hips and legs are the motor of the clean, and the back is the transmission; a slipping clutch (i.e., bent arms or soft back) means lost power at the wheels.

It makes sense to me to separate the learning of the squat and the squat clean. Think of the power clean as the separator, if it helps. I think the result will be a better squat, and just as useful a clean. Now, you don't have to listen to me, but if I were you I'd listen to Bill.

The Power Clean

Strong Enough?

"Exercise ferments the humors, casts them into their proper channels, throws off redundancies, and helps nature in those secret distributions, without which the body cannot subsist in its vigor, nor the soul act with cheerfulness."

Joseph Addison (Circa 1700)

Personal Equipment:
The Good, the Bad, and the Silly

There is very little personal equipment that is absolutely necessary to take to the gym. But it is surprising how much stuff some people carry with them. An old can of Desenex, three half-used rolls of athletic tape, a dog-eared copy of *Fear and Loathing in Las Vegas*, a pair of oddly-stained shorts, several wrap fragments of various lengths, one band-aid, and a chalk can are among the items in my old gym bag under the desk now. I have seen troll dolls, leaky tubes of Icy Hot, very old packages of Honey Buns, cans of sardines, "lucky" shirts in need of washing, "lucky" socks in need of throwing away, and a pair of aluminum hooks with wrist straps attached so that hand strength could be completely eliminated as a criterion for the successful execution of any exercise. As a general rule, some equipment is useful, some equipment is most definitely not useful—and in fact is a bad idea—and some is just absurd.

In order of most useful to most silly, in the gym bag we have squat shoes, chalk, a lifting belt, straps, knee wraps or knee sleeves, wrist wraps, elbow wraps or sleeves, gloves, devices such as a "Manta Ray" or a "Sting Ray" that hold the bar for you, and anything you intend to use to shave anything but your face.

I had a member named Lonnie a while back. Nice guy, lovely wife (whom he met there in the gym), and strong under the bar, but with a few annoying habits. One day I walked out of the office and saw him doing incline leg raises on the incline sit-up board, holding on to the bar behind his head with his hands *strapped to the bar.* I, of course, approached him to question this behavior. He said that he was using straps so he could concentrate on his abs better, which is, he said, very important in an ab exercise. I made fun of him for several weeks while he was there to train, putting a strap on when I turned a doorknob, strapping on to the bar for a bench press, coming out of the bathroom with one strap on my right hand, sweaty and breathing hard, going out to the truck and strapping on to my steering wheel, until I got tired of it. Lonnie never seemed to think it was as funny as I did, but he quit using straps for things that don't require straps.

Straps are a good example of equipment you need for some things but shouldn't use for others. Straps are good for heavy shrugs, the kind that are done in the rack with a hundred pounds more than your max deadlift; very heavy shrugs are not possible without straps. They are good for deadlift assistance stuff, like rack pulls from below the knees to lockout that can be done with weights too heavy to hold for a set of five. They are not good for your max deadlift, because at some point you actually have to make your grip strong enough to do one. And there is absolutely no excuse for doing your pull-ups with straps. If your grip strength is the limiting factor in your pull-ups, your deadlifts will fix that soon enough. If you see anybody strap onto a dumbbell for any reason, you know you are watching a person who thinks in terms of muscle groups and who does not think about performance.

Performance-based training depends on all the components of the systems involved to carry their share of the load. The best way to train all these systems is in the context of the task they are expected to perform. One of the worst ways to train them – possibly worse than not training them at all – is to separate them out and train them individually. There is more involved in performance than the strengths of the individual components of a movement. The effective, efficient integration of these components – a.k.a. *skill* – is the most important aspect of their cumulative action, more important even than strength alone, because skilled people are better at sports than people who are merely strong. Almost invariably, the unnecessary use of equipment interferes with the development of this integration of systems because of the imbalance in strength it causes, which in turn directly interferes with the expression of skill.

Straps illustrate this concept well. The terminal end of the kinetic chain in most sports is the hand. No sport that I am aware of allows the use of straps, and they would actively interfere with many. Straps replace grasping strength. If this function is prevented from being developed while doing the movement in which it is used, well, you can see the problem.

A heavy shrug in the power rack is a useful exercise for a powerlifter working on the finish of the deadlift. In this case, the straps aid in an assistance exercise that is not possible to do without them. Straps might be useful in the case of a hand injury, a cut or a finger injury that renders a necessary exercise undoable otherwise. Olympic lifters like to use straps at times, especially for snatches, which tend to destroy hand skin when done several times a week. Any assistance movement that *can* be done without them should be, and certainly any core exercise like deadlifts should be done, at least most of the time, without an aid that would leave an important component undeveloped.

Strong Enough?

Since it's been mentioned, competitive powerlifting uses a lot of equipment. I'm not referring to this, but rather the adoption of an equipment dependency by people not going to a three-lift meet where equipment – for better or worse – is a part of the sport. Since non-competitors don't usually invest in a $300 bench shirt, we'll assume you haven't.

Squat shoes are the single most useful piece of personal equipment you can own, and the only one that is really, honestly necessary. It only takes one set of five in a pair of squat shoes to demonstrate this convincingly to anybody who has done more than one squat workout. Squat shoes form a stable position from which to drive, because they are built on a non-compressible wedge of wood or leather, and in my opinion are absolutely essential for all squats and all pulls from the floor, as well as presses. Running shoes are designed to squish, so as to absorb the shock of impact during thousands of repeated bodyweight footfalls, and wearing them to squat is nearly equivalent to squatting on your bed. Cross-trainers are very little better, and those horrible "shocks" things are the very worst in existence. Training barefoot is preferable to these kinds of shoes, and barefoot is not good: things get dropped in a gym that can be hard on feet, even feet protected by shoes; platforms can shed splinters; your injured feet will bleed; blood is a pain in the ass to clean up.

Any shoe with a compressible heel will not be a stable platform for any barbell movement with a ground-reaction component, since the first part of the force applied to the ground is absorbed in the shoe. What's worse, they absorb an unpredictable amount of the force in an unpredictable direction each time, depending on your exact position over the center of gravity of the system, making you pay a dear price for very tiny differences in form each rep. Squats are hard enough anyway without making each rep a completely different experience because of your shoes.

Hell, dress shoes are better than running shoes, and many records have been set in work boots. The problem with boots is that the tops restrict ankle movement, and while that's not a huge factor in the squat, a pair of low-quarter squat shoes allows you to squat *and* do all the Olympic lifts that require more ankle mobility. Most squat shoes have metatarsal straps to increase lateral stability and suck the foot back into the shoe to reduce intra-shoe movement.

The problem with squat shoes is that they are never available at the shoe store in the mall and can be obtained only from weightlifting equipment suppliers. But they are not that expensive, especially when compared to new name-brand basketball shoes, they last for years if you don't act like a dork and wear them anytime other than when you're training, and they make the most important lifts in your program safer and more efficient. Get some.

Chalk should be provided by your gym. It makes your grip more positive and less likely to slide on the bar, and therefore safer and more efficient. It reduces callus formation, making it easier to manage your calluses so that they don't tear. If your gym doesn't provide it, ask them why. If they don't allow you to bring it, training is not their priority and maybe you should be somewhere else. I don't train without my shoes or chalk. Really.

Now the controversy begins. A belt is one of those things that some people say is always a crutch, a bad unnecessary thing that keeps your abs from getting strong. Does its use prevent something from strengthening? I don't see how, and I personally am one of those old guys who is still able to squat and pull because the belt allows me to stabilize my torso enough to do so, despite numerous back injuries. If I don't belt, I can't squat more than about 185. So, you want me to quit training because I'm old and beat up?

Look at it this way: a belt stabilizes the spine by adding to the intra-abdominal pressure provided by the abs, so a belt is like extra abs. Extra abs allow more weight to be squatted and pulled, thus placing extra stress on the prime movers and on the spine, and thus requiring that more work be done by all of those systems. If they all do more work because of the heavier weight, they all get stronger, even under the belt. It is always smart to do as many warmups as possible without the belt, but if you are squatting heavy and are going to use a belt, put it on for the last warmup as well as the work sets, because it changes the movement pattern a little. And if you can squat heavy without one, do it, but be aware that you can always squat more with a belt, and there may come a time when this is important. If you need a belt, wear one; if you want a belt, use it when appropriate and be aware of how it works.

An often overlooked function of the belt is the proprioceptive feedback it provides, telling the body about tightness and position because of its pattern of contact with the skin. Even when worn loosely it performs this function. Knee wraps function the same way when worn loosely. Wraps are commonly found in many gym bags. Both knee and wrist wraps may have a place in that bag, depending on how and when they're used. Knee wraps are most usually three inches wide and six feet long, and the kind made for powerlifting are very thick and strongly elastic. These are designed specifically to resist knee flexion, and are thus aids to extension (a squat suit works the same way, by resisting hip flexion). But they have other uses, as in my situation where I have no ACL in my right knee and have had some work done on my left patellar tendon. I use them below the patella, loosely wrapped to keep things a little tighter, and provide some feedback about position. They are on loosely enough that I can leave them on the whole workout with no discomfort or venous occlusion – nothing south of the wrap changes color. Used in this way, they add support and a feeling of tightness that actually helps with position, but no assistance with the weight itself. In fact, they are quite helpful to me in managing my patellar tendinitis since the wrap absorbs some of the stress and keeps things warm, and I'd recommend them to other old guys if you've had as much knee trouble as I have but still want to train relatively hard.

Knee sleeves are the stretchy little rubberized cloth jobs that work like loose wraps. But you'd better keep them washed between workouts if you're as prone to skin problems as I am. They don't breathe at all, and it took me exactly 45 minutes to develop a rash under them one day, a cute little situation that lasted about a week. Use some bleach in the water.

The wrong way to use wraps would be to put them on tight enough that they need loosening between sets. This level of support is quite different from the loose way. My loose wraps allow me to squat without further injury; tight wraps allow a lifter to squat *more weight*. They add greatly to the rebound out of the bottom normally provided by the hamstring/adductor stretch reflex. This is different from the function of a belt, in that a belt makes no direct contribution to actually getting the weight back up. If you are not going to a power meet, you are fooling yourself about how much you squat if you use wraps this way. Fooling oneself, of course, is not good; it leaves one more prone to being fooled by others.

Wrist wraps are useful too, since wrists are commonly injured joints. A wrist injury really screws up a clean or a snatch, and can hurt on a squat if the bar is held incorrectly. In these situations, a wrist wrap is necessary and good. But as a fashion accessory, they are for dorks. I don't know that they keep anything from getting strong, but there is just something offensive about wearing unnecessary gear that is designed for use by somebody that is not you. If you're not an injured Olympic lifter, or you derive no benefit from wearing a wrist wrap, leave it in the bag until you are or do.

Elbow wraps are a little less commonly seen, since no powerlifting federation allows them for the bench press, but the same thing holds true for them as for knee and wrist wraps: good if used appropriately, bad if relied on for pounds on the bar, silly if worn because you think they look cool. One of the problems with elbow wraps is that when the elbow is in full flexion, the bulk of the wrap between the bicep and the forearm tends to "jack" the joint apart and produce a shearing force on the ligaments. This is uncomfortable in the bench press, press, back squat, front squat, and when racking a clean, and most people try them a couple of times and quit using them for this reason, even though they can be helpful on rather rare occasions when no acute elbow flexion is to be done.

Personal Equipment

Gloves are used by serious lifters only in the event of a skin injury to the palm of the hand that a glove would allow to be trained around. Under no other circumstances do I want to see "weightlifting" gloves on anybody, not even a maxillofacial surgeon or a church organist. Not even a lawyer. Gloves add a layer of unstable material between the bar and the hand, destabilize the grip, prevent necessary callus formation, and actually make gripping harder due to the effective increase in diameter of the bar being held. Fat bars are used for this reason to work the grip, but gloves are not. Gloves are annoying. Inexperienced, non-serious people think they are supposed to wear them because they see them in the fitness magazines. Cindy Crawford wears them. Richard Simmons wears them. I'm sorry, I just can't talk about this anymore.

And those devices that hold the bar on your back or your shoulders for you, well I can't stand to talk about them either. Except to say that anyone who uses them should be beaten with a hammer, out in the parking lot.

Look, get some squat shoes and use them. Get some chalk if your gym doesn't have it, or get another gym. Get a belt; use it when you need to. Get some wraps if you need them, but not if you don't. And if you just *have* to shave anything but your face, do it at home, okay? Unless you're Cindy Crawford.

Strong Enough?

Going Deep

Anyone who says that full squats are "bad for the knees" has, with that statement, demonstrated conclusively that they are not entitled to an opinion about the matter. People who know nothing about a topic, especially a very technical one that requires specific training, knowledge, and experience, are not entitled to an opinion about that topic and are better served by being quiet when it is asked about or discussed. For example, when brain surgery, or string theory, or the NFL draft, or women's dress sizes, or white wine is being discussed, I remain quiet, odd though that may seem. But seldom is this the case when orthopedic surgeons, athletic trainers, physical therapists, or nurses are asked about full squats. Most such people have absolutely no idea what a full squat even is, and they certainly have no concept of how it affects the knees, unless they have had additional training beyond their specialty, which for the professions mentioned does not include full squats. Because if these people knew anything about squatting, and the difference between a full squat and any other kind of squat and what they do to the knees, they would know that "full squats are bad for the knees" is wrong and thus would not be making such ridiculous statements.

The squat referred to here is the full, below-parallel squat, the style that is – at least theoretically – performed at a powerlifting meet, where the top of the patella and the iliac fold (the crease in the shorts that defines the position of the hip joint) form a plane below which the hips must drop. In a correct full squat, the femurs will be in line with the feet, the

63

heels will be about shoulder-width apart and the toes pointed about 30 degrees out from straight ahead, so there is no twisting on the knee. The knee will be just a little in front of the toes, no more than an inch or two, and the weight will be distributed evenly on the feet, with heels most definitely down. With the back tight and flat, the torso will lean forward enough that when the bar is on the shoulders, a line dropped plumb from the end of the bar to the ground would go through the middle of the foot; this usually puts the back at about a 45-degree angle with the floor.

Now, this is not to say that doctors, PTs, and nurses haven't been exposed to knee anatomy. They have, but they have not been exposed to correct squatting, and thus they have no idea how the movement is related to knee anatomy. The fact is that the knee and hip anatomy actually *dictate* correct squatting technique. Smart as these people are, you'd think that they could figure this out, and thus derive correct technique, the way we ignorant, uneducated lifters have. But I guess you'd be wrong if you thought that.

What generally happens is that when one of these professionals explains why you will die if you do squats, he will demonstrate with squat technique so incorrect that even unweighted it hurts to watch, and then he'll say SEE THERE, SQUATS ARE BAD FOR YOUR KNEES. This is like saying that if you burn the beans, they stink up the house, so you shouldn't eat beans. You don't get to define the argument in terms that prove you're right, and then charge money because you won the argument.

The problem is that, as is so often the case, one profession does not recognize that the other has something to offer. Or more correctly, as in this case, that the other is even a profession, with a body of professional knowledge and experience that is particular to it. Chiropractors, optometrists, and pharmacists often dislike doctors for this reason. Granted, a chiropractor who claims to be able to treat cancer might be causing his own problems, but it would be better if doctors recognized that chiropractors have a legitimate, useful place in the health care professions. And that strength and conditioning professionals, with decades of experience in getting people strong, might know more about squatting than people whose training has been in the treatment of injuries and disease.

Maybe it would be useful if I didn't alienate all the orthopods and PTs in the world with a blanket indictment of their perspicacity. But hey, tit for tat—*they* have indicted the single best, most valuable exercise in the weight room, the one more athletes have used to get strong and advance their careers than any other, and I can be petty at times. Anyway, what are *they* going to do about it? Make me squat?

I had a conversation with an athletic trainer at a recent coach's convention. He explained that he didn't like his coaches teaching the squat because they were bad for the you-know-whats. I showed him how I coach the squat – femurs and feet parallel, hips back and deep, heels down, as earlier described. He said, "Well, if you do them like that they're okay. But these guys can't teach this to the kids." I asked why not, and he said "It's too hard to teach!" I said, "I just showed you. Did that seem hard?" His first problem was that he didn't know what constituted a correct squat. His second problem was that he didn't know how to teach the coaches how to do it, much less how to teach them how to coach it. When he realized that he had just learned how to teach them, since he had just learned himself, his problem became the fact that he had painted himself into a corner with his previous position. The kids are the ones who lose in such a situation.

The fundamental misunderstanding here is about what we're trying to accomplish when we squat. The quadriceps are not the only muscles that are supposed to be involved in the exercise. The hamstring muscles on the back of the thigh attach at the front of the tibia, at the bottom of the knee, wrap around it on both sides and pull back on the knee from below it as they get tight. The adductors connect the groin area of the pelvis to the medial (inside) aspect of the femur, and these muscles also pull back on the knee when they tighten, but from above the knee and toward the inside. Both of these muscle groups tighten from behind the knee as the torso leans forward, the knees travel out to stay parallel to the feet, and the hips reach back for correct depth, balancing the forward-pulling stress from the quadriceps and the patellar tendon around the front of the knee. But they only exert this balancing pull *when they are stretched*, in the full squat position. At the bottom of the squat, where the hamstrings and adductors are fully stretched, there is as much pull on the knee from the posterior as from the anterior. In this position, the quadriceps' knee extension force is balanced by the hamstrings' knee flexion force. At the same time, the adductors (on the inner thigh) have stretched too, and if the knees stay parallel to the feet, as they should, the adductors will get tight and pull on the femurs. This knee-out position anchors the femur so that adductor contraction and hamstring contraction produce hip extension—a little hard to visualize, but apparent enough when sore adductors show up the day after a heavy squat workout.

Because the hamstrings attach to the pelvis at the ischial tuberosity, any forward tilting of the top of the pelvis will stretch the hamstrings away from their insertion points at the knee. When the pelvis and the back are properly locked in a flat rigid unit by the back muscles, the forward angle of the torso and pelvis tightens up the hamstrings. At the same time, if the knees are shoved out to the sides at the bottom of the squat, not forward over – or, god forbid, inside – the toes, the adductors are tightened as well. (Sorry this is so complicated.) If this is done correctly, there is a slight "bounce" or muscular "rebound" off the hamstrings and adductors at the bottom of the squat, which initiates the upward drive out of the hole. This hip extension (the standing up out of the squat) is accomplished much more efficiently and much, much more safely for the knee when it occurs from this correct position—*a position that cannot be achieved unless the squat is deep.*

The below-parallel position accomplishes more than just knee safety and lifting efficiency. It allows the squat to be quantified. If every rep is below parallel, then every rep represents the same distance traveled with the load. If the load increases, and the distance the load moves is the same, then moving it requires more work. But if the load increases while the squat depth decreases, the work performed is not necessarily greater, and may in fact be less. Without knowing how far the weight traveled, it is impossible to say how much work was done and, consequently, whether any improvement took place since the last workout. If every squat is correctly below parallel, then every squat is safe, efficient, and comparable with every other squat a person does. All the hip and leg muscles can be trained, joints can be protected, progress can be made and judged, programs can be evaluated, and contests can be held without fistfights breaking out.

Strong Enough?

The part that puzzles me is, what do *they* think happens during a half squat? Good things? The only muscles under any stress are the quads, since the hamstrings, glutes, and adductors are not involved due to the limited range of motion. The spine is invariably loaded too heavily, since it is incredibly easy to "squat" big weights if you have to move them only a few inches. The knees are disproportionately subjected to anterior stress, since the lack of depth does not engage the hamstrings and activate their posterior balancing effect. The lower back muscles, used in the full squat to maintain spinal alignment and the back and pelvis angle, get little work in the half squat because it is not deep enough to ever put the low back at much of an angle. So, if half squats are dangerous for the spine and the knees, and fail to train most of the muscles of the hips, legs, and lower back, why do *they* always tell you to do them? Because they just sound like a better idea? And where did *they* get the idea that squats were bad in the first place?

I can answer that last one. It was Dr. Karl Klein's study at the University of Texas in 1961, a poorly designed and badly conducted mess that has never been replicated and has been successfully rebutted many times. Klein concluded that below-parallel squats produced "loose" knees, although no other training protocol was evaluated for comparison, no other tester administered the measurements, and all the data was biased by pre-test questioning of the subjects. To me, the interesting question is why the findings appealed to so many people, and why they made an impression that has persisted for fifty years.

I think I can answer that one too. Half squats are easier than full squats. They are not as much work, in both the physical and moral sense. People are lazy. So, half squats are appealing. Even people who claim they are squatting deep are often not, since depth is sometimes hard to self-assess and since it is easier to squat high. This is deep psychology here, brain stem-deep. Full squats run contrary to human nature. But – and this is a very fundamental question – who is in charge? You, or your brain stem?

Are you willing to let medical professionals make excuses for your lack of willingness to do the hardest, most productive exercise in the weight room, an exercise that has been proven safe by decades of use by millions of very strong people? I don't think you are. Please prove me right.

Strong Enough?

A New, Rather Long Analysis of the Deadlift

Proper deadlifting technique is that which allows the most weight to be lifted. This rather straightforward observation is true because the mechanics that permit an efficient heavy deadlift are the same for all weights, light or heavy. Why would 500 lbs. be pulled one way, and 400, or 200, or 88 another? The pull from the floor is a basic function of human skeletal and muscular anatomy, and is controlled by the physics that operate this system of levers. This is obviously true, but less obvious is why.

Many years ago I was strong. Well, relative to what I am now, I was strong. It is a rather dim memory, but I have pictures and trophies that I am told are mine. At the time, I was a decent deadlifter, usually among the last few even in our state-level meets to open, usually with something close to 600 lbs. My PR was 633, done on two separate occasions at a bodyweight of 220. The deadlift was really the only thing I did well, at least on the platform. My training buddies and I trained it hard, probably twice as much as other lifters spent on the lift.

In the early 1980s there were no deadlift "suits"; we wore plain wrestling singlets (we even wore them on our five-mile barefoot walk to school in the snow; I know how it sounds, just bear with me). Wrestling shoes had just become popular, the reasoning being that the shorter heel decreased the distance that the bar had to be pulled. I found that I could pull more effectively in my squat shoes, with the heel helping me more effectively push the bar away from the floor using my quads in the initial knee extension. We were doing an exercise called halting deadlifts that involves only this initial push off the floor. Haltings start from the same position as the deadlift, with the back locked and the shoulders in front of the bar, and come up to a point right above the kneecap. The keys to the halting were the push of the feet against the floor – the knee extension – and keeping the shoulders out in front of the bar which, when done correctly, could be felt in the lats almost as much as chin-ups. This was important, although at the time I didn't know why.

We also began using another exercise we called the rack pull. The haltings worked from the floor up, and rack pulls fill in the top part of the pull. They start from pins set inside the power rack right below the level of the knee, at about the tibial tuberosity, and move up through lockout, finishing in the same position as the deadlift. The emphasis in the rack pull was the locked back and the hip extension, with an attempt to actively exclude any knee extension from the movement. The start position for the rack pull is also out over the bar, but as the bar comes up past the knees the chest comes up as the hips begin to bring the back into the vertical finish position. The overlap between the two movements at the knee ensured that there was no "hole" in the training of the full deadlift with these two partial exercises. We didn't feel the rack pull in our lats that much, with me again not knowing why, or even thinking about it.

But very good questions can be asked here. In both exercises, the start position involves the shoulders being in front of the bar, which is to say, on the other side of the bar from the rest of the body. The interesting thing about this position is that when you're in it, your arms are not vertical.

They are at about a 10 degree angle from vertical, because the shoulders in front of the bar have them reaching back to the bar at this angle.

But it sure seems as though they would almost *have* to be vertical since a damned heavy weight is hanging from them. Shouldn't they hang straight down?

And another thing: shouldn't the back be as vertical as possible, since vertical is easier on the back? If the shoulders are out in front of the bar, the back will most assuredly not be very vertical. It might even be nearly horizontal, almost parallel to the floor, if you have short arms or long legs. But vertical is easier, because the more vertical the back is, the less torque, the rotational force applied against the lower back, will be produced. In a system in which mean old Mr. Gravity provides the force, the closer to vertical the force is applied, the less of the force is converted to torque. Torque is 100% of the force when applied at 90 degrees – your back bent over parallel to the floor. And there is no torque when the force is applied parallel to the lever arm, when the back is vertical, where it is all simply compression. The closer to vertical the back is, the smaller the effects of the lever arm formed by the rigid back with a weight hanging from the top of it.

The answer to both is no. The arms cannot hang straight down; they must be at an angle from the shoulders back to the bar, and the back cannot be vertical if the shoulders are in that position. But why is this true?

This has bothered me for years in a very quiet little squeaky way, the question usually behaving itself and not demanding an analysis. Recently I have been dragged to the board and forced to think about it more thoroughly. You

73

tell me if I got it right. If I didn't, you'll need to tell me why. And if you already know all this – and you very well might – just stop reading now because this is going to be pretty dry.

The force that is transferred from the back to the bar doesn't just leap over to the arms through the air. It is transferred to the arms through the shoulder blades, and it just so happens that when the correct deadlift position is assumed, the shoulder blades are in fact directly over the bar in a line perfectly plumb and vertical to the bar. Let's review the basic force-generation mechanics of the deadlift and see if this makes any sense.

The force that makes the bar go up is generated by the muscles that extend the knees and the hips, and this force is transferred up the rigid spine, across the scapulas to the arms and down to the bar. The elbows obviously have to be locked for the force of the pull to get to the bar efficiently, without being partially absorbed by the biceps, so we'll assume that the arms are always straight. The weight leaves the floor when the quadriceps extend the knees, but for this to happen the hamstrings and glutes must anchor the hip angle open. The hamstrings pull down on the pelvis from below, and the glutes hold it from the top of the iliac crest; if the back stays flat this allows the force to travel up the rigid back held at a constant angle while the quads push the floor. This knee extension can then provide the initial drive off the ground. If the hip angle collapses during this initial push, which happens when the hamstrings and glutes fail to hold their position, the quads don't contribute to the movement of the weight since they straightened out the knee without any movement of the load. When this happens, you have just shoved your butt up in the air without the quads lifting any of the weight. Done correctly, the hip angle opens only

very slightly as the bar rises to the knees and the back angle –
the angle the torso makes with the floor – stays constant.
During this process, the quads move the weight, the glutes
and hamstrings hold the hips down, and the flat back
transfers this force up to the shoulder blades and down the
arms to the bar. If the knees extend without moving the bar,
the movement becomes a stiff-legged deadlift, with the glutes
and hamstrings doing all of the work without the help of the
quads.

At the starting position, the bar must be as close as
possible to a position directly over the middle of the foot,
where the force acts against the ground: it must be in contact
with the shin, and this point must be over the middle of the
foot. If it is contact with the shin but *behind* the mid-foot,
this would mean that the hips are too high, the shins are too
vertical, and the knees are too straight, in a stiff-legged
position with the quads already shortened. The correct back
angle that uses the quads most effectively off the floor will
have the shins inclined forward to the point at which the bar
will be touching them directly over the middle of the foot.

In fact, the bar must stay in contact with the legs all
the way up to lockout, since the farther away from the knee
and hip joints it is, the longer the lever arm – the one
mentioned above – is, producing more torque against the
hips. The most efficient starting position for any pull from
the floor is *always* one in which the bar is in contact with the
shins over the mid-foot. This is another problem with
raising the butt up without moving the bar: the knees pull
back as the butt raises, pulling the shins away from the bar
and leaving it too far away from the point of ground
reaction.

Strong Enough?

In the correct starting position, the scapulas are directly over the bar. This is because the force transferred up the spine is distributed to the scapulas from the ribs against which they lie flat, sprung from their posterior attachments against the spine and supported through their curvature around to their anterior attachments on the sternum. They are held fast by the trapezius muscles, which attach the spine of the scapula – the long bony ridge extending down the length of this otherwise broad, flat bone – to the vertebral processes along a broad origin that extends from the top of the neck well down the middle of the back, and the rhomboidius muscles which form a narrower attachment between the medial edge of the scapula and the spine. The scapulas have only a muscular attachment to the back; they float within their muscular base to allow a range of shoulder position. The retracted position, the one in which they are pulled closest to the vertebral spine, is the position of maximum muscular tension, and maximum support from the traps and rhomboids. It is the position in which they can most effectively receive the force from the back for transfer to the arms. At the start position the inferior part of the muscle, the part furthest down the back, is the main contributor to the retraction of the scapulas; the upper part becomes important at the top of the deadlift.

The shoulder blades are the skeletal components that receive the force from the back and change the direction of the force from parallel to the back angle to one that connects with the bar. So they are the components that transmit the pulling force to the gravity that the deadlift must overcome. Gravity acts perpendicular to the floor, so the scapulas must be perpendicular to the bar, because the weight actually hangs from the scapulas.

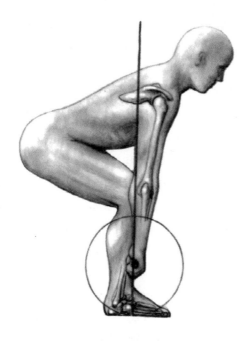

Of course, this position is ultimately dependent on the ability to keep the spine in rigid extension during this process. If the muscles that keep the spine rigid are not contracted properly or are overcome by the load and pulled into a position where the spine is rounded, three problems result. First, the intervertebral discs are not designed to bear weight effectively anyway. This bipedal stance we occupy is rather poorly thought out, and discs are better at just separating bones than forming a weight-bearing surface between them. They only bear weight well when they are in the correct position, where the surfaces of the vertebrae they separate are oriented in the way the disc is shaped for them. This position is achieved when the back is in extension, both lumbar and thoracic. This is the normal anatomical position for the back, and the one in which the spine must be maintained by the back muscles during a deadlift or any other lift involving force transfer up the spine. Injuries are prevented when this position is maintained.

Second, if the back fails to maintain extension during the deadlift, some of the force that would have gotten to the bar had the back stayed in extension gets absorbed in the lengthening muscles, and lifting efficiency is reduced. If the back rounds enough, an erect position cannot be attained at the finish, since the function of the spinal erector muscles is to maintain rigid extension, not to actively extend the spine under a load. So, the correct starting *and* maintaining position for the back is *always* one of spinal extension for the whole back.

Thirdly, there is the problem of shear. Shearing force is an internal force that acts in a tangential direction to the segment on which it is applied; it results in a sliding-apart. Shearing force is applied to the spine during the deadlift, and results in a tendency for the vertebral segments to slide apart along the plane of the discs. But shear is not a problem as long as it is effectively overcome by the isometric contraction of the spinal erector muscles working with the intrathoracic and intra-abdominal pressure generated by the anterior trunk muscles. Possibly the most important function of the trunk muscles is the elimination of the shear force on the spine, accomplished when these muscles maintain the spine in perfect rigidity. It is for these reasons that the deadlift is regarded as the best back exercise in existence.

In their retracted position, the scapulas lie at an angle that puts the glenoid – the cup that articulates with the ball of the humerus – slightly forward of the spine of the scapula. This means that in the deadlift starting position the top of the arm at the shoulder will be slightly forward of the scapula. If the scapulas are directly over the bar and the shoulders are slightly forward of it, there is a slight angle from the shoulder to the bar, and the arms will not be vertical. This is where the lats become important. If the shoulders are in front of the bar, the back is flat, and the bar is touching the shins, this angle is inherent in the position. Tension from the lats keeps the bar from swinging away from the shins into a difficult pulling position. The lats keep the bar vertically under the scapulas – over the mid-foot – so that force can transfer to the bar in an anatomically efficient way, and so that the distance between the bar and the point of ground reaction is the shortest.

The lats are good at this. They attach near the top of the humerus along a broad, flat insertion, and in the starting deadlift position the most lateral fibers of the muscle are at about 90 degrees to the bone. This is a very efficient position for maintaining tension on the bone. If you tie a long rope between a tree and a car, you can pull the car by pulling on the rope at right angles – 90 degrees – to the rope. This works best if you are in the middle of the rope, but we are not trying to actually *move* the bar back, just keep it against the shin until the bar is above the knees. The halting deadlift, since it works the part of the range of motion that involves this lat function, has a profound effect on lat strength and development when done with heavy weights.

After the bar passes the knees, the knee angle has opened up quite a bit and the hip angle begins to open as the function of the hamstrings and glutes changes. As the bar rises above the knees, the torso becomes more and more vertical as the lift gets closer to the finish position. The hamstrings and glutes begin to actively extend the hips,

changing both the hip angle and the back angle. At this
point most of the knee extension is finished and the hips are
catching up. During this phase the scapulas rotate back to a
position behind the arms as the chest comes up. They have
moved from directly over the bar to behind it as the torso
becomes vertical, and the traps change their support from the
inferior portion of the muscle to the superior, the part visible
above the shoulder. The lats drop out of active participation
in the lift since they are no longer required to keep the arms
from swinging away forward. As the lockout portion of the
lift is approached, the knees and hips have both moved
through the hard part of their respective ranges-of-motion, a
little more being left for the hips to do than the knees. Their
final lockout will occur simultaneously. At lockout, the
shoulders are back, the knees and hips are extended, the spine
is in normal anatomical position with chest up, face straight
forward, lower back locked, and everything stable.

So, with these things in mind, there are three criteria
for a correct starting position for the deadlift. The back must
be locked in extension, the bar must be touching the shins
over the middle of the foot, and the shoulders must be out in
front of the bar so that the shoulder blades are directly
vertical to the bar with straight arms. It doesn't matter what
the individual looks like in this position as long as these three
criteria are satisfied. Legs may be long or short, the back
may be long or short relative to the legs, arms may be long
or short, a kyphosis may be present, and these factors will all
influence the appearance of the starting position, primarily
through varying the angle the back makes with the floor.
But as long as all three of the criteria are satisfied, the starting
position is correct. As a coach, you should become familiar

with the effects of the anthropometric variables on starting position, and learn to tell wrong from merely weird.

In both the halting deadlift and the rack pull the shoulders start out in front of the bar, because both exercises start with the bar below the knees where the scapulas are still over the bar. The halting stays in that position all the way up and down, whereas the rack pull rotates out of it shortly after the knee is cleared. And now I know why. And I'm as sorry as you are that it took so long.

Strong Enough?

Training Advancement & Adaptation

The most fundamental concept in exercise is *adaptation*, the response of the human body to physical stress. And the most fundamental concept in exercise programming is the way adaptation varies among athletes at different levels of training advancement. The only thing hard to understand about them is why these two perfectly obvious principles go largely ignored by the vast majority of people who practice within the field of exercise programming. Strength coaches and personal trainers, exercise physiologists, physical therapists, and athletic trainers routinely "plan" exercise programs for people with no regard for these most logical and obvious derivatives of the basic nature of animal physiology. This must stop. We will stop it now.

The term "stress" is quite familiar to those of us with a job, responsibilities that are sometimes difficult to fulfill, or three girlfriends. In physics, stress is the force which causes deformation in a system, and the deformation is referred to as "strain." The stress may be the force of a snatch dropped on the platform from overhead, and the strain may be a bent Eleiko bar (but wait, that *cannot* happen). In physiology, stress is that which causes an adaptation in a system. The adaptation to the stress of a shovel handle might be calluses where the handle rubs. But blisters might also form, which would indicate a stress that exceeds the immediate capacity for adaptation. Notice that neither calluses nor blisters form on the other side of the hand – stress, and the adaptation to it, is specific. The phenomenon of adaptation to stress was first described in 1936 by Dr. Hans Selye in a paper that appeared in the journal *Nature.* The basic gist of the paper is that when stress is applied to a viable physiological system, the response is either adaptation through supercompensation (calluses when the stress is of a magnitude that can be adapted to) or a failure to adapt (blisters where the calluses would have formed if you weren't so pig-headed about insisting on wearing your gloves). In dire circumstances, failure to adapt means the death of the organism. For athletes, it usually just means overtraining, a mere inconvenience in the grand scheme of things unless an endorsement or a pro contract is lost in the process.

So, the process by which strength and performance are accumulated is one of stress and adaptation. As is true with most systems that improve with accumulated change, the farther away from the predetermined limits of potential improvement the system is, the more easily and rapidly the system improves. And conversely, the closer the system is to that limit, the harder and slower improvement occurs. Predetermined limits to improvement within a mechanical system are due to the physics that govern the operation of the system; for a physiologic system the limits are genetic.

In either case, the approach to these limits is asymptotic: the closer you get to the limit, the harder it is to get closer, the longer it takes, and the more it costs in terms of effort and (usually) expense. The time between not knowing how to write your name and being able to compose a complete paragraph is only about six years; it has taken another forty or so to achieve the high pinnacle of literary ability evidenced herein by your author. A much, much, *much* better illustration is automotive performance. Factory spec is often 130 mph these days, with 160 attainable with the purchase of some extra stuff. If 180 is the goal, way more stuff is necessary, and 185 requires more stuff than most people can afford; 200 is unattainable by a production chassis and drive train.

This is an example of the principle of diminishing returns, immediately recognizable in nature as a rather common thing. It applies quite specifically to physical training, and is obvious to anyone who has trained athletes through the progression from novice to advanced. Novice trainees get strong/fast/quick/agile/skilled very rapidly, intermediate-level trainees improve more slowly, and advanced athletes, who have begun to closely approach their genetic potential for development and improvement, progress even more slowly.

If we are going to postulate a pattern of approach to a predetermined genetic limit, we'd better define what a genetic limit might be. Genetic potential could be understood as the inherited ability to adapt to a certain level of imposed stress, a capacity that will permit a commensurate level of performance. Individuals with a high level of genetic potential to perform under particular types of stress can excel in sports or activities that demand a high level of adaptation to those stresses. A person with a high percentage of fast-twitch muscle fiber, a dense neuromuscular system (a high density of motor neurons to muscle fibers), advantageous anthropometry that provides for efficient leverage against external resistance, a natural psychological capacity for pain tolerance and adherence to a task (personality being a strongly genetically-influenced trait), and a good enough cardiovascular capacity to function under the conditions that exist at high peak loading would be said to have "good genetics" for Olympic weightlifting. This same genetic profile in a person of exceptional size, with the added benefit of big hands and an ability to handle a lot of Scotch whisky, would indicate "good genetics" for Highland Games competition. Conversely, a person with a high percentage of slow-twitch fiber, a naturally high aerobic capacity (composed of several different characteristics that contribute to the ability to transport and metabolize both O_2 and metabolic substrate), an average stature and fine skeletal structure would have "good genetics" for race walking. Genetic potential is specific to the activity that the genetic capacity predisposes toward. Quite obviously, the more pronounced the degree of skew toward either the aerobic or anaerobic end of the metabolic continuum, the less capable the individual would be at anything else. Elite weightlifters make lousy marathon runners, and this is good.

Many individual aspects of performance ability are a function of genetic endowment. Neuromuscular quality is probably the easiest to observe. The ability to recruit motor units into contraction is largely determined by the number of motor neurons that are hooked up to the muscle fibers and the percentage of these fibers that are classified as type IIb, the permanent fast-twitch variety. This morphological feature cannot be altered by training any more than eye color can. Vertical jump is an excellent test of this inborn characteristic, and kids with very efficient neuromuscular systems will display an above-average vertical jump at an early age. Individuals with a preponderance of slow-twitch, sparsely-innervated muscle will display poor vertical jumping ability forever, and no amount of training can change this. A person with a 10″ vertical will never have a 30″ vertical, and most likely never even get to 15″. My guess is that vertical jump can be improved about 25%, but I'm not a track coach and other more qualified people might have a better handle on it. But I'll bet I'm not far off.

The principle of diminishing returns leads to some obvious conclusions about training. For instance, changes in the rate of progression from novice to advanced might not be quite so obvious to coaches who work only with advanced athletes, since they have no experience with the process. The strength coach who has developed his programs having only worked with college athletes at the D1 level may very well have no appreciation of the fact that most 15-year-old kids can add ten pounds to their squat every workout for two months, and should do so to take advantage of this ability while they have it. The strength coach who started at the college level and moved to the rather rarified ranks of professional sports may be under the impression that machine training is actually useful for sports performance. Such a coach has never worked with anyone other than advanced or elite athletes of exceptional genetic potential and therefore sees a decidedly unrepresentative sample of the population. He may very well have no idea of the vast gulf that separates exceptional native ability from performance earned the hard way by those of more average genetic capacity—people he'll never see on his team. He may actually think his athletes are strong because his one-set-to-failure Hammer Strength machine program works so well.

It is also true that the novice trainee who can add weight to each barbell exercise every workout is wasting time if this does not occur. The first part of the progression from novice to advanced takes place quite rapidly, precisely because the organism is so thoroughly unadapted to any stress at all. The difference between a completely unadapted trainee and that same individual at his advanced level varies with the genetic potential of the individual ("advanced" refers to training history, not absolute performance), but in every case the unadapted individual makes progress rapidly *because any stress at all will cause an adaptation.* Riding a bicycle will improve the rank novice's bench press, and jogging three miles will improve his squat, even though this obviously daft approach would never work for a more adapted trainee and would never work very long for anybody. Novices respond to everything precisely because they haven't adapted to anything yet, and any stress, even what will later be considered the wrong stress, will cause an adaptation toward greater fitness.

Couple this with the fact that novices are not strong enough to use weights heavy enough to prevent rapid recovery (unless heinous abuse by an inexperienced or insecure coach occurs), and you have the perfect recipe for rapid progress.

This quite easily demonstrated fact has caused a lot of silly research to draw a lot of ridiculous conclusions. If your study population is untrained college freshman males with no previous sports background enrolled in a weight training class for the first time who volunteer for the study because they fit these criteria and are being given a better grade for participating, I submit that *any* exercise protocol you try on them will work pretty damned well. If your study population is untrained sedentary adult females between 55 and 65 years old, leg extensions and leg curls might very well appear to work (at least for strengthening the quads and hamstrings) as well as "squats." This is especially true if you think that "squats" are done to a nearly—but not quite—ninety-degree knee with the toes pointed forward while looking up at the ceiling, inhaling on the way down and exhaling on the way up. (It pisses me off even to write this.)

The progression from novice to advanced must necessarily go through an intermediate phase, during which some of the characteristics of novice-level adaptation ability are lost on the way up toward the limits of genetic potential. Novice training properly takes advantage of the unadapted organism by using rapid linear increases in training loads for the major exercises. The novice can recover well enough between workouts that more weight can be lifted each time, and is not strong enough to exceed his recovery capacity under the conditions that allow linear progress to occur. During this period, both strength and the ability to recover and adapt are developing. But when enough progress has taken place that the amount of work that can be administered during one workout is insufficient to stimulate further progress, and when the amount of work that *would* stimulate progress cannot be recovered from between two workouts, the trainee is an intermediate. At this level, the trainee has developed the ability to apply enough stress to the system that a longer period of time is required for recovery than the two-day period between two workouts. Intermediate training utilizes weekly organization rather than workout-to-workout increases, enough time to apply sufficient stress to cause an adaptation as well as sufficient time for recovery.

Advanced athletes are those for whom more complex training than the weekly programming of the intermediate is necessary. They have chosen a sport in which they compete and are actively trying to win those competitions. Advanced athletes have made the commitment in time, money, and personal sacrifice for the sake of athletic excellence, and they have progressed to the point that the limits of genetic potential must seriously be considered, in terms of what can be accomplished and what the athlete is willing to do to accomplish it. Complex manipulation of all training variables is necessary to ensure the continued ability of these athletes to make progress; this progress is hard won and even harder to keep. The advanced athlete walks a razor-thin line between training at a level high enough to progress in tiny steps toward the best performance possible and the quite high probability of injury, overtraining, or both.

Most trainees are novices, since at any given time the greatest majority of the training population has just started. The sad fact is that 95% of all the people who start training with weights never advance beyond this level, most likely because their training is not managed correctly at this time, and they do not get the results they both want and need to stay motivated to continue. Novices make the most progress most rapidly; most of the people who ever lift weights will make most of the progress they ever make during the novice period of their training. Intermediate level trainees have specialized their training toward a sport or training style, and advanced athletes are by definition competitors in a sport; the vast majority of the human race will never achieve this level of training advancement, and has no desire to do so. So novice training is, and always will be, the most important training you either do or teach others to do.

These are the consequences of the fact that your response to training depends on where you are on the road from novice to advanced. Any plans, programs, or projections made without recognition of this fact will not work as intended. Any research conducted without deference to this fact is invalid. Most importantly, any athlete trained without respect to these principles will fail to achieve what he is capable of.

Strong Enough?

Conventional Wisdom and
the Fitness Industry

Glenn Pendlay and I were talking one evening about the prospects of making a living in the fitness business. He was finishing his masters in exercise physiology and wondering aloud about his options. I was providing the witty repartee and the beer. At the time I had been in the industry in some capacity for 23 years and a gym owner for 17 – although any realistic assessment would have to conclude that, if earning lots of money were the criterion, I had not been terribly successful, so we were mainly discussing his situation.

"I don't know if I want to work in this industry," he said.

"Why not?" was my insightful, probing response.

"Because the general public doesn't know the difference between me and you and the kid at Gold's."

"Well, nobody's stupid enough to confuse me with you, but you may have a point about the pinsetter."

"You know what I mean." And I did. "The average person trying to make a decision about where to spend their money on a gym membership or personal training has absolutely no way to tell the difference between a coach with our experience and the kid that Gold's certified last weekend."

"Yeah, that's a pain in the ass. And the pinsetter has better arms too."

"And abs. How are you going to explain to a 42-year-old salesman in a midlife crisis that the kid at Gold's has abs because he's skinny and 19? And that he really shouldn't worry about abs right now? I mean, I'm a trainer, you're a trainer, and the kid is a trainer, and of the three of us who looks the most like a trainer?"

"Well Glenn, I guess you need to give me 20 situps."

This is a real problem for the fitness industry. Even among the state-licensed professions, there are glaring examples; every town has an embarrassingly bad doctor, lawyer, dentist, and architect who somehow manages to make not just a living but a good one. The obvious answer is that *caveat emptor* applies, always and everywhere – except that it doesn't. People trust authority, even when it is unearned and undeserved.

As Dan John says, the pinsetter does have "Trainer" embroidered on his polo shirt.

But what about when he has "Doctor" written on his shirt? Or "Physical Therapist"? Or even "Chiropractor"? These health care professionals have no specific training in sports performance or strength and conditioning, yet they frequently practice in this field as the patient is on the way out the door: "You don't need to lift heavy weights for what you want to do anyway. Just do lighter weights for higher reps." Without the slightest idea whatsoever about what they are saying. And since these people have the state's stamp of approval and charge more than I do, they usually get listened to a lot more carefully. The public perceives medical professionals as the ultimate authority on all things having to do with the human body. This is frequently unwarranted.

It wouldn't be so bad if they said things that made sense, or asked us what to say since we are supposed to be familiar with this material. But they'll still tell you, right here in the twenty-first century, that full squats are bad for your knees, that weight training will jeopardize your son's career in sports, that long slow distance is necessary for "being in shape," and that one day on/one day off is always the best schedule. I do not practice orthopedic surgery. I claim no expertise regarding pulmonology or obstetrics. In a perfect world, those who do would not attempt to practice my profession in the absence of relevant training and experience.

The media feed this situation, precisely because they like to be fed themselves. The Noon News exists in the realm of the 60-second canned story, the gist of which is condensed into a simple, un-nuanced explanation of the bleeding obvious, and which always prominently features the considered opinion of an M.D. who wants you to see him before you start any exercise program, possibly for some reason that might involve a co-pay. The mainstream print media are no different, except that they can waste more of your time with longer stories. The reporters, anchors, and journalists that glue this mess together have no particular expertise in exercise, biology, or, really, anything else except presentation. Space is available, it must be filled, and that which comes from a medical professional is assumed to be correct. This bias is then transmitted to the general public and reinforced every time the TV is turned on or the Health section of the newspaper is opened.

The really weird part of this is that these medical people typically form their impression of what constitutes fitness from the very media they influence. Doctors, again having no specific training in exercise, come from school with only the information they have been able to obtain on their own. The most effective orthopods are often former athletes, who learned from coaches and personal experience about how the human body adapts to stress. But most did not, and so most get their information from the same people their patients do. This is indeed a sorry situation.

Further complicating this matter is the sad fact that the academic exercise science community is also in the business of conventional wisdom. Biomechanics/kinesiology/exercise physiology/physical education has contented itself for many years with creatine studies and peer review of each other's work. For example, Volume 20, number 4 of the NSCA's *Journal of Strength and Conditioning Research* published a total of 42 papers, five (12%) of which list the editor-in-chief as a co-author, and 17 (40%) of which list associate editors (the ones doing the peer-reviewing) as authors, either singly or in groups. One associate editor is listed on five papers. Another associate editor has 11 of his 14 published papers (according to the National Library of Medicine's catalog) published in the *JSCR*. The editor-in-chief has published 11 his past 25 authored or co-authored articles in this journal. This level of cronyism is not the norm for most reputable peer-reviewed scientific journals, most of which are concerned less about the number of papers they publish and more about their quality and academic reputation.

And it does affect the quality of the publication. Volume 20 of the *JSCR* contains a peer-reviewed study that determines that the best direction to look when squatting is up, but it fails to include a description of the exercise; the actual method used to squat might be germane to the topic, you'd think. There is a peer-reviewed study of the effects of bands on the squat that uses a Smith machine for the exercise. There is a peer-reviewed study on the effects of different pacing strategies on the 5-km running event that uses a *treadmill* instead of a track or road. Another peer-reviewed study compares the effects of super-slow training with volitional speed training—in other words, super-slow vs. no particular speed, which is unable to conclude anything except that super-slow doesn't work very well when compared to anything else. There is even a study that probably should have appeared in the journal *Duh* that demonstrates that step aerobics does not improve vertical jump or power production. The NSCA's other peer-reviewed publication, the *Strength and Conditioning Journal*, ran an amazing article a few years ago by one of their state chairmen that advocated a program for – I am not making this up – periodized abdominal training.

The big-box health club industry at large is the concentrated, stinking sum total of this silly bullshit. The industry-standard floor configuration is 55 percent of the space in treadmills and the latest fashion in "cardio" equipment. Closing The Sale is the only valued expertise on the staff. Deadlifts and chalk are prohibited, sweating is discouraged, and noise is considered offensive. Squats and presses are understood to be Smith machine exercises. There is probably a wrist curl machine. The two-year contract sticks it all together.

This mass of conflicting information has produced confusion in the general public about whom to listen to, whom to take seriously, and whom to pay. It has also produced a population that is unimpressed with the fitness industry, a population that is fat, diabetic, lazy, and convinced they can never be anything else. All the aforementioned problems within the industry have contributed to the lack of results that would tell them otherwise.

Government licensure has been suggested as a remedy for the widely varying quality of exercise advice. But this is absolutely the last thing that legitimate practitioners should ever want. If the government grants your trainer's license, and the government gets to administer the test and thereby set the standards for practice, who will get to tell the government whether full squats are in fact bad for the knees? Or whether it is safe to work at intensities above 75 percent of "max" heart rate? Not the folks taking the test, most certainly. Because after all, doctors know more about this than *anybody* else. What do you think they'll say? And when we're all operating under the same standards of practice, your license will depend on your adherence to them, not on your ability to produce results for clients and trainees. Think long and hard about this one.

So how do you inform an uninformed public? How can you communicate the not-too-complicated-but-more-complicated-than-Sudoku concepts of human adaptation to physical stress, and the real exercise that relies on these concepts, to people not equipped with the information and experience to understand them?

Well, how did Covert Bailey manage to convince everybody that dietary fat was the equivalent of rat poison, even though they most definitely did not want to hear that? How did Kenneth Cooper get everyone in any field that involves wearing a white coat to believe that exercise *equals* long slow "cardio"?

Through endless repetition, that's how. Through the conversion of one person at a time. After all, LSD (long slow distance) does work better than absolutely nothing, and enough people lost enough weight and gained enough fitness with jogging and a low-fat diet that inroads were made. Stories were written, TV specials were filmed and repeated, jogging became the exercise of choice in movies and television shows, and doctors told their patients. The public schools and universities and public health services incorporated the LSD paradigm into their curricula. Thirty years later, here we are.

We have a harder job than they did. Squats, sprints, and carb control are not as comfortable and easy as jogging and Snackwells. But our type of exercise has always worked; since Sparta, people have been getting out of their training exactly what they put into it. I didn't invent squats, Coach Burgener didn't invent snatches, and Coach Glassman isn't the first to use chins, cleans, and burpees in a single short, hard workout. Many generations of people have learned the same things we know and have done the same things we do. The difference now is the media, which have caused two new things to happen. First, people are now more aware of their health and how the things they do affect it than ever before. This is good. But, second, the media want the things they say to be believed so they can retain their *gravitas*, and easy things are more likely to be believed than hard things. So while they have focused attention on health – and, by extension, fitness – like never before, their version of fitness is just silly, incapable of producing compelling results for anybody except the most detrained people. And then the medical community, probably in an effort to follow the modern version of Hippocrates' maxim ("First, do not get sued"), picks up this ineffective, sub-adaptive approach to fitness and makes it THE LAW under color of authority.

Our job can be done the same way they did theirs. First, we continue to get superior results for our trainees. Working with high-profile trainees is quite helpful, since they are the focus of media attention. But word-of-mouth is even more necessary; people are influenced by what they see and read, but their personal acquaintances and friends make a greater difference in their perceptions of things like this. The more people learn from us and grow stronger, healthier, and more capable – and easier on the eye – the less difficult our job will be. When the weight of experience begins to tip public perception in our favor, the media and the healthcare profession will also alter their perception of what works and what doesn't. Just keep doing what's right, like you would anyway.

"So I guess we're both screwed, huh?" I asked Glenn.

"Not me," he said. "I'm going to cut in line. I'll get in the barbell business."

"Hmm. Maybe there's an angle there. Maybe I'll write a book."

Strong Enough?

"The history of our race, and each individual's experience, are sown thick with evidence that a truth is not hard to kill and that a lie told well is immortal."

Mark Twain

"There is nothing new under the sun but there are lots of old things we don't know."

Ambrose Pierce

Popular Biomechanics

The most useful theories are those that simplify our understanding of apparently complicated things. The theory of evolution explains the rather interesting fact that frogs and humans both have two forearm bones, that grasshoppers and catfish share the common pattern of repeated trunk segmentation, and that all of us, including bacteria, use pretty much the same high-energy phosphate system to move things around inside our cells. My observations will never be this profound, interesting, or important. They will not even be that original. But since you apparently have nothing better to read right now, let's just enjoy these next few minutes together as though they will be useful.

Barbell training has been the focus of my attention for the last couple of decades. I am not bored with it yet. Whenever I have the opportunity to train a group of interested, motivated, bright people, I learn as much as they do. It has recently come to my attention that there are objective ways to describe proper form for the basic barbell exercises that are valid for everybody that does them, regardless of their anthropometry. For example, it doesn't matter how long your femurs or how short your back, the bar is going to come off the ground in a deadlift when the bar is directly under the shoulder blades. This position will place the shoulders slightly forward of the bar and the arms at a slight angle back to it. This is a function of the mechanics of the skeleton, and is true even when form is bad: if the bar is too far away from the shins, and not right against them in a position that minimizes the torque against the hip joint, the bar still leaves the ground from a position plumb to the scapulas. Even if you wanted your back vertical due to the mistaken idea that a vertical back is "safer" than an inclined back, ultimately it doesn't matter because your skeleton cannot pull a heavy weight this way. But any *correct* pull from the floor – for deadlift, clean, or snatch – will start with the bar directly under the scapulas and against the shins. Any video of a heavy deadlift, clean, or snatch from the side will demonstrate this fact. It will also show that the bar leaves the ground when it is right above the middle one-third of the foot.

Why the middle one-third of the foot? Because the weight of the load is distributed over the whole plantar surface of the foot if the load is in balance, and the load in question is the combined weight of you and the bar acting at the ground directly under the center of mass (COM) of this lifter/barbell system. If the weight is disproportionately on the toes or heels, the COM is either forward or behind where it should be to achieve even distribution against the ground. When the weight is light, the mass of the body is the primary factor in balance. As the bar becomes heavier – as you get stronger – it becomes a larger percentage of the load, and the COM of the system gets closer to the COM of the bar. For this reason it is possible to do light weights with form that will be wrong, or ineffectual, at heavier weights, but heavy weights are unforgiving of errors in form that result in unbalanced loads.

It is also a fact that a squat is only in balance when the bar is directly over that same middle one-third of the foot. It doesn't matter where the bar is on your back or shoulders, if the bar is moving straight down or up as it will in any heavy squat that doesn't get dumped on the floor, the bar will never deviate much from a position directly above this place. If it does, it gets out of balance and slows down until it either gets back in balance or gets missed.

With this in mind, it is possible to identify certain aspects of any correct squat, regardless of bar position.

At the top of the squat:
- All the skeletal components that support the bar—the knees, hips, and spine—will be locked in extension so that the muscular components have to exert only enough force to maintain this resting position
- The bar will be directly over the mid-foot

At the bottom of the squat:
- The spine will be held rigid in lumbar and thoracic extension
- The bar will be directly vertical to the middle of the foot
- The feet will be flat on the ground
- The thighs will be parallel to the vertical plane of the foot
- The acetabulum, or hip joint, will be lower than the top of the patella

Now, you're free to deviate a little between top and bottom, but if you don't start and stop as described, you're wrong mechanically and the squat will be harder than if you were right. And, actually, if the bar stays in the correct vertical position over the mid-foot on the way down and up, you are doing it right. Your skeleton is solving the problem of how most efficiently to use your muscles to get the job of squatting done. It does so within the constraints imposed on it by the physics of the barbell/body/gravity system we all lift within. (And no, this does not vindicate the Smith machine. There is a gigantic, bottomless ocean of willingly misunderstood difference between a machine that makes the bar path vertical and a squat that is executed correctly enough to have a vertical bar path. Muscle, skeleton, and practice should do the job of keeping the bar path vertical, not grease fittings and floor bolts.)

If the bar path is vertical, two other squat variables can be analyzed. The angle of the back – that is, the general plane of the torso – will vary with the position of the bar on the torso, either on the back for a back squat or on the frontal deltoids for a front squat. And the position of the knees – the front-to-back distance from the back of the butt to the front of the knees – will vary with both back angle and stance. If the above five non-varying criteria for bottom position are met, bar position and stance will control all the other position variables in all styles of squat.

The position of the bar on your back determines what the trip down and up will look like from the side. In a deadlift, the bar is always hanging from the arms and is always under the scapulas until it passes the knees, so the back angle is essentially predetermined, though of course it varies according to individual anthropometry. But the front squat, high-bar back squat, and low-bar back squat are all done with different back angles. Each causes the skeleton to move in a different way between the top and the bottom of the movement. This is because the bar position on the trunk varies relative to the hip and knee. When the bar is on the back, either on top of the traps in the high-bar or "Olympic" squat or just below the spine of the scapula in the low-bar squat, the back will be inclined forward at an angle that will place the bar over the mid-foot. The higher the bar on the back, the more vertical the back angle will be to make this happen. This means that a high-bar squat must have a steeper back angle than a low-bar squat if form is to be correct. A front squat places the bar at roughly the same level as a high-bar squat, but across the depth of the chest on the anterior deltoids, requiring the back angle to be so steep as to approach vertical if the bar is to stay over the mid-foot.

A near-vertical back will result in a knee position much forward of that in a low-bar back squat; the high-bar squat is intermediate between the two. A knees-forward back-vertical position at the bottom produces a more acute knee angle, an already shortened hamstring, and a more extended hip. The front squat is therefore a much more quad- and glute-dominant movement than the low-bar back squat, since these are the muscles that remain in a position to contribute to the lift. This is also what's wrong with knees too far forward in the back squat: it is undesirable not so much because having the knees too far forward will destroy them, but rather the detrimental effect it has on hip extension.

The vertical back position of the front squat seems like it would result in a more direct compressional load on the spine than the back squat's inclined angle would produce. This is partially true. The lower back is in a nearly vertical position, but the upper back has a much tougher job because the load it is holding up is farther away from the spine. The bar in a back squat – low-bar or Olympic – sits directly on top of the muscles that are holding it directly over the mid-foot. The front squat places the bar all the way across the depth of the chest, which in a bigger guy might be 12 inches away from where it would be sitting in a back squat. This is a much longer lever arm than no inches at all and presents a mechanical challenge to the muscles that maintain thoracic extension – the upper portion of the longissimus dorsi and the serratus anterior muscles. It is very common to get pretty sore between and just below the shoulder blades when first starting the exercise. So while the lower back is vertically compressed, unless you are flexible enough to be capable of actually leaning back a little with the bar on your anterior delts, your thoracic erector muscles have a lot of work to do. This results in a gradual shift from compression to torque from low back to upper back, so things are not as simple as they may seem. The load on the lumbar spine in the front squat is friendlier (partly because it will be lighter), as long as the upper erectors are able to maintain position, and for this reason many people find it easier on the low back to front squat. And anything that gets too heavy gets dropped automatically before death can occur.

The upshot of all this technical analysis is that back angle in the squat is determined by bar position. But wherever the bar is on your back, it will be right over the middle of your foot, and your feet will be flat on the floor, or your mechanics will be less than efficient.

Another immutable criterion for correct form is that your thighs will be parallel to your feet. This keeps the feet flat, removes any non-linear loading (twisting) of the knees, and ensures the participation of the adductors in the lift if the stance is wide enough to require it. Toe angle – and therefore knee angle if the feet are parallel to the thighs – is determined largely by stance width. A close-stance squat can be done either with toes out or toes pointing forward with only a slight angle, maybe just five or ten degrees. But the knees have to travel straight forward to keep the thighs parallel to the feet; the knees always follow the toes to preserve the linear relationship between the patella, the patellar tendon, and the tibial plateau. These three things need to stay in a nice straight line if the knee is to continue to work without undue wear, especially under a load. And this is why the knee voluntarily lines up this way in any unweighted squat. Next time you stand up from a seated position, like next time you take a crap, verify this for yourself (anything to make a point, eh?).

The wider the stance, the wider the foot angle and the wider the knees will have to be to keep the thighs parallel to the feet. At closer stances, with more forward-pointing toes, the knees will travel farther forward than they do at wider knee angles. This is because the narrower the stance, the longer the distance from the front of the knee to the back of hip along the sagittal axis. And the longer this distance, the more the knees must travel forward to accommodate it. A close stance with toes pointed out will display the same knees-forward position that a moderate stance at the same foot angle will. At very wide stances like those favored by powerlifters using squat suits, there is very little forward travel of the knee at all, and the shins tend to stay nearly vertical. But a wide stance will not work if the toes are pointed forward, because of the twist it places in the knee; this is about the only squat stance that is really anatomically wrong. I prefer heels at shoulder width for the generalized effects, but other stances can be used correctly as long as the knee is not twisted.

Feet flat on the ground are another important indicator of balance, and the coach learns to look for "air" under the heels as a sign of subtle mechanical problems. Most people who squat in those stupid "shocks" running shoes have learned how to squat balanced on the ball of the foot out of necessity, so it can be done. The point is that optimum engagement of the hip extensor muscles, the "posterior chain," cannot take place in this position, and that is what makes it wrong (that is also what makes weightlifting shoes a good place to spend a little money). Lots of form problems get embedded in lots of motor pathways; the reason we are having this discussion about objective technical markers for good form is to help identify the why and how of correct. Feet flat on the ground are absolutely essential for the engagement of all the muscles that make a squat correct. And "flat" refers to the pressure of the weight distributed evenly across the sole of the foot, not the angle of the foot against the floor that might well be the product of the shoe.

The depth of the squat is determined empirically by observing the relationship between the hip joint and the top of the patella. These landmarks are easy to see from the side: the hip joint is behind the apex (the most pointy part) of the folds in the shorts made when the hips bend, and the top of the kneecap is clearly visible on the knee even through sweats. Depth is important for hundreds of reasons you already know, so I won't go into it here. Just remember: if in doubt, it's high. Ass-to-ankles is not absolutely necessary, and if it requires a relaxation of the lower back arch to get there, it's wrong. Breaking the plane of parallel is good enough, deeper is better, but excessive depth to satisfy an arbitrary ideal that cannot be attained with useful weights is counterproductive.

The press can be described in a similar way.
In the starting position for the press:

- Knees, hips, and lumbar and thoracic spine are all locked in extension
- The bar rests on the deltoids or chest, or is a least below the chin, depending on individual flexibility
- Elbows are in front of the bar
- The bar is directly over the mid-foot

At the top of the press:
- Knees, hips, lumbar and thoracic spine, and elbows are all locked in extension
- Scapulas are elevated (i.e., "active shoulders")
- The bar, the scapulas, and the mid-foot will be vertically aligned

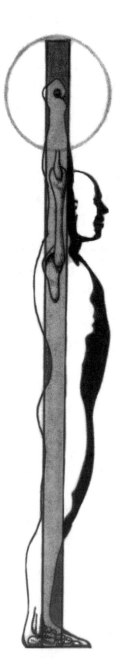

Strong Enough?

During the trip up from the starting position to the top, the bar path should also be vertical and directly over the mid-foot. If it deviates from this position a little as it travels forward around the head, the COM is kept over the mid-foot by leaning back slightly, to the extent necessary to balance the bar deviation. This should be minimized by keeping the bar close to the face during the press so that the bar doesn't get so far away forward – thus increasing the length of the lever arm between the shoulder and the bar – that it cannot be pressed efficiently.

The clean and the snatch are more complicated than the slow lifts because they travel so much farther and utilize movement around so many joints. But like the press, any deviation of the bar from alignment over the mid-foot is compensated for by movement of the body that keeps the COM of the system in balance over that point. Both lifts start and finish with the bar in the same relationship to the mid-foot that the other barbell exercises do, with a bunch of added complexity in between to keep the bodybuilders away from the bumper plates. Any discussion of the subtleties therein is best left to my betters.

The point of this rather dry discussion is that there are objective ways to quantify proper form in the basic barbell movements, to allow us to understand better what we're seeing when we watch people lift. These criteria are based on skeletal considerations that do not vary with anthropometry, even though the individual expression of these criteria will. There are many ways to screw up the lifts, but an understanding of what we should be looking for at crucial places in the movements reduces the number of ways we are likely to do so. It also gives us some objective anatomical data to on which to base our discussions of good form and best practices for lifting.

"I wonder if other dogs think poodles are members of a weird religious cult."

Rita Rudner

Sex, Appearance, and Training

To quote a famous fitness author, "Women are not a special population. They are *half* of the population." But they respond to heavy physical stress differently than the other half of the population. Despite this fact, women get the best results when they train for performance, because even though there are differences between men's and women's response to training, there is no difference in the quality of the exercise needed to produce the stress that causes adaptation. In other words, silly bullshit in the gym is silly bullshit, for both sexes.

The women's "fitness" industry has been around a long time. "Figure salons" were common in the 1960s, and my first job in the industry in 1977 was at a club that alternated hours for men and women. We had separate staff, with the women's shift working Monday, Wednesday, and Friday and the men's staff basically working Tuesday, Thursday, and Saturday, which pretty much precluded any 3-on/1-off training. But the women didn't *train* anyway. They exercised, toned, firmed, and sculpted. They were required by the club to train in tights (which the club sold), and sweating was strongly discouraged because exercising this hard was 1) apt to build bulky muscles, 2) caused the exerciser to make too much noise and that, combined with the sweat, might 3) intimidate the other ladies.

At the time the men's "program" wasn't much better, but training hard was a matter of pride in the Nautilus room and our members suffered from no lack of effort or exertion; rather they were the victims of our staff's inexperience and ignorance of exercise science. The women's program suffered from an entirely different problem: the perception that women were absolutely, inherently, and permanently different from men to the extent that any program of physical exercise had to be different from men's programs, right down to the molecular level. Both suffered from an emphasis on appearance (typically "masculine" or conventionally "feminine") rather then performance.

Men and women do in fact respond differently to training, but not in the ways that the industry, the media, and popular culture have presented as fact. Furthermore, and quite importantly, both the real, actual differences and the ridiculous, supposed differences between men and women have created a lot of the aforementioned silly bullshit in the gym, the net effect of which has had a particularly detrimental effect on women's training.

Women's collegiate and professional athletics and its participants have for many years held the answers to the questions most women ask about exercise, answers that have gone fastidiously ignored by the figure salon industry. The results, in terms of both performance and aesthetics, admired by the vast majority of women had been and continue to be routinely produced by advanced athletics programs, yet "body sculpting" sessions – low-intensity machine-based circuit training classes, the 1980s equivalent of most modern Pilates and yoga classes – were the approach sold to the public. Now, as then, "easier" is easier to sell.

The fact is that aesthetics are best obtained from training for performance. In both architecture and human beauty, form follows function. Always and everywhere, the human body has a certain appearance when it performs at a high level, and depending on the nature of that high-level performance, this appearance is usually regarded as aesthetically pleasing, for reasons that are DNA-level deep. The training through which high-level performance is obtained is the only reliable way to generate these aesthetics, and the only exceptions to this method of obtaining them are the occasional genetically-gifted freaks – people who look like they train when they were just born lucky. As a general rule, if you want to look like a lean athlete – the standard that most active people strive to emulate – you have to train and eat like an athlete, and most people lack the "sand" for that.

Despite this unfortunate truth (most truths seems to fall into this category), the fitness industry continues to sell aesthetics first, as though it is independent of performance. The focus is always on appearance, as though that can actually be trained for. Think about it: how many sets and reps do you do, and with what weight, to make your quads just *look* better? I know how to make your squat stronger, but how do you program Bun Blaster sets and reps for a tight ass? Exactly how does one go about obtaining a great glute/ham tie-in? I may be able to double your number of pull-ups in a month, but I don't know how to give your back that V-shape everyone craves without increasing your pull-ups. Every single aspect of programming for resistance training that works at all does so because it increases some aspect of performance, and appearance is a side-effect of performance. Appearance can't change unless performance does, and the performance changes are what we quantify and what we program. We pretty much know how to improve that, but the industry is based on the fiction that appropriate training proceeds from an assessment of aesthetics. Your appearance when fit is almost entirely a function of your genetics, which are expressed at their best only when your training is at its highest level, and this level is only obtainable from a program based on an improvement in your performance, in the gym or on the field. And the best improvements in the gym occur when participating in a program that looks more like performance athletics—the kind of training done by competitive athletes – than one that looks like waving your arms and legs around on a machine or slowly rolling around on the floor.

With that in mind, and counter to the conventional industry wisdom, here are some more unfortunate truths:

- Your muscles cannot get "longer" without some rather radical orthopedic surgery.
- Muscles don't get leaner – you do.
- There is no such thing as "firming and toning." There is only stronger and weaker.
- The vast majority of women cannot get large, masculine muscles from barbell training. If it were that easy, *I* would have them.
- Most women who do look like men have taken some rather drastic steps in that direction that have little to do with their exercise program.
- Women who claim to be afraid to train hard because they "always bulk up too much" are often already pretty bulky, or "skinny fat" (thin due to a lack of muscle) and have found another excuse to continue life sitting on their butts.

- Only people willing to work to the point of discomfort on a regular basis using effective means to produce that discomfort will actually look like they have been other-than-comfortable most of the time.
- You can thank the muscle and women's magazines for these persistent misconceptions, along with the natural tendency of all normal humans to seek reasons to avoid hard physical exertion.

You already know all this, or you wouldn't be reading at this rarified level. All enlightened physical culturists of the twenty-first century know that women and men train basically the same for performance improvement and the resultant physiques. But significant differences do exist between men and women in terms of performance and real strength and conditioning training for that performance. This is why men and women do not compete against each other in varsity and professional sports. These differences must be understood and appreciated if training programs for women are to be realistic and effective.

It is ironic that the most pervasive fear voiced about barbell training by women in the general public is the very thing which is prevented from happening by the primary factor distinguishing men's and women's performance abilities. Women don't get big muscles because they don't have the hormones to build them, and differences in hormone profile between men and women are the primary reason that male and female performances are different.

Strong Enough?

There are several aspects of female performance that are different from those of men, all of which depend on neuromuscular efficiency, and all of which are a direct result of lower testosterone levels and the effects that testosterone has on motor unit recruitment, central nervous system excitation, and other neuromuscular factors. These endocrine/neuromuscular effects, more than any social factors resulting from differences in upbringing, account for the differences in male/female performance; social factors can be overcome, physiology cannot.

For instance, women can perform a 5-rep max lift (5RM) with a higher percentage of their 1RM than men, because they cannot as efficiently demonstrate absolute strength at the level of 1RM intensity. I have observed this in the gym repeatedly over decades of working with motivated female athletes. A max single, carefully titrated up to failure with small incremental increases for an accurate and precise measure of where that max actually was, always turned out to be much closer to the previously determined 5-rep max than experience with training men would suggest it would be. Quite frequently, her 1RM was only seven pounds heavier than her 5RM. This seemed strange at first, but I eventually quit arguing with the universe and learned to take this into account when testing and programming trainees.

It is also germane to handling lifters at meets. I made a terrible mistake many years ago at a powerlifting meet with a third-attempt pick for a female lifter. It was too heavy because I had based it on her second attempt as though she was a he, and she most definitely was not. If a 5RM is closer to a max single in women than men, a 2RM – a decent second attempt deadlift – is too. She missed that third attempt and first place as a result of my inability to better apply what I actually knew, and I'm still sorry, Rosellen.

This important difference in the expression of strength is most likely the result of the efficiency with which motor units can be recruited, an ability associated with the neuromuscular effects of testosterone on nervous system function. It is displayed in essentially all vertebrates and recognized throughout zoology as a predictable factor in animal behavior.

Women can also continue to produce eccentric contractions after concentric failure long after men fail eccentrically. This is probably because they have less completely fatigued themselves at positive failure, and subsequent negatives are not being done from as depleted a position as a male's would be. Several years ago I was training a gal who thought she might like to be a bodybuilder, and we were playing around with some seated behind-the-neck presses one afternoon. She was fairly strong and was doing a high-rep set with 75 pounds. She had done nine reps done when I decided to see how tough she was. She got to failure at ten, about where I had guessed she would, and I started giving her negatives – helping her from the bottom back up to lockout and letting her lower it under control. I expected her, like an average guy, to get another three or four. After she did *15 more* and finally slowed down to where I could call her set finished, I decided she was pretty tough. But later, after other women showed me the same ability, I decided she was about average for a fit woman.

This is caused by the same neuromuscular factors that control concentric strength expression. The ability to create very high levels of motor unit recruitment also produces the capacity to create commensurately high levels of fatigue. If you use up all your ATP doing concentric work – because you can produce enough contractile intensity to do so – you won't have enough left to do many more eccentric contractions, and vice versa.

Explosive movements such as vertical jump that demonstrate power and its requisite high levels of motor unit recruitment are very typically performed by women at lower levels of proficiency than men of the same size. Field events, tennis, basketball, weightlifting, and all sports that inherently involve an explosive performance component, exhibit a high degree of sexual dimorphism, to the extent that the best women in the world can often be beaten by varsity high school or college freshmen and sophomore men. Cyclic activities that require high levels of motor unit recruitment at short repeated intervals, like sprinting and sprint cycling, also display sexual differences. The effects of testosterone are indeed profound, and often tempting.

In addition to these neuromuscular effects, muscle mass differences between men and women explain the profound disparity in upper-body strength between the two sexes, even among equally well trained and conditioned athletes of the same size. These differences are due entirely to differences in testosterone levels. Throwing, pressing, upper-body lifting at work or in training for other sports, as well as gymnastics, golf, and swimming all display marked differences in performance between men and women.

In fact, the extent to which the gap in performance between females and males of comparable body weights narrows is generally explainable by a higher-than-usual testosterone level in that particular female. This may be due to exogenous hormone administration (the magazine way) or naturally-occurring abnormally high levels. Or it may be due to an adaptation to continued high levels of workload through an increase in endogenous production of either testosterone or dihydroepiandrosterone sulfate, a slight increase that beneficially affects recovery and performance without the pubescent-male side effects. The data on this is not terribly good, but then again, neither are the studies, which tend to use isolation machine exercises as the stressor.

There is such a profound difference in male and female testosterone levels that the strength differences between men and women are almost entirely accounted for by hormone level, whereas the differences among males – say between pro athletes and actuaries – are, while hormonal to a certain extent, more attributable to other factors.

Such big differences in male and female performance might seem to bolster the fitness industry's position on the necessity of sex-specific programs, exercises, and facilities. But I already bragged on your enlightenment, and we all know that it makes as little sense for women to exercise in ineffective ways as it does for men. This is due to the fact that sexual differences do not constitute a major division in physiology that rises to the level of zoological; men and women are not as different as, for instance, sea anemones and wombats. Anabolic hormones are very powerful substances that effectively enhance performance. They are banned by the USOC for this reason, not because they are dangerous. Hormones administered to two otherwise identical organisms can cause major changes in the organisms' morphology, but these changes are still pretty much just a matter of degree, not of basic pattern. Men and women both recruit motor units into the same patterns of muscular contraction, albeit at different levels of efficiency. Physiologically, Andy Bolton and your grandmother operate the same way, in the same sense that Great Danes and Chihuahuas are both dogs. In both cases, stress demands a response, and that response is determined by the basic physiology of the organism. It is the degree and efficiency – not the nature – of that response that varies with the hormonal status of the organism. Testosterone produces a more robust strength-enhancing response, and that is why testosterone and its analogues are often used by athletes to enhance training. Gentlemen, I suppose this means that we are cheating.

It also means that the type of stress that causes the most profound adaptation will be the same for both sexes, and only the degree of the adaptation will vary. Squats work better for everybody than leg extensions, leg curls, and Bun Blasters because of the quality of the stress they produce. Squats are performed with the same muscles by everybody, they are hard for everybody, hard enough to produce system-wide stress for everybody, and this is why they work for everybody. Men are more efficient at responding to the stress of squats in terms of elevated testosterone levels, and in this respect men can get stronger and bigger faster than women. But women aren't served well by using less efficient ways to produced stress because they respond to it less efficiently. On the contrary, a less efficient stress response means that it is *more* important to use quality training methods. It must be listed with the Unfortunate Truths that squats are still the best exercise for women to train with barbells, just like they are for men.

Barbell exercises that demand strength, balance, power, coordination, and mental focus produce a type of stress – and therefore a type of adaptation – that is superior to either low-intensity floor exercise or isolation-type machine exercise. The stress is the stimulus that causes the adaptation, and the quality of the adaptation is thoroughly dependent on the quality of the stress. An exercise that does not involve balance cannot cause an improvement in balance. Likewise, if bone density, power, agility, coordinated strength, and mental focus are parameters that need improvement, the stress that causes the adaptation must specifically tax those parameters or they will not adapt. This simple fact is ignored – or perhaps more realistically, misunderstood – by the marketing geniuses that run the fitness industry, and thus the value of squats, deadlifts, presses, cleans, and combinations of barbell movements with gymnastics skills and track and field athletics goes unappreciated.

It would also complicate business. It's very hard to find staff qualified to train members at optimal levels of skill and intensity. (Hell, it's hard to find people who will just come to work.) And it will be as long as the standard employment model of the industry is the minimum wage college kid. Qualified coaches generally get paid more than health clubs are willing to spend, and as long as the public demands no more it will get no more. If prospective members got in the habit of asking for functional training, the industry would shift in that direction. As long as the market for treadmills and Pilates is strong, that's what will be for sale; when intense, effective exercise becomes more popular, the market will find a way to offer it. Right now it seems that education might help solve the problem.

There are signs that this paradigm may be breaking down. As CrossFit, Velocity, and other performance-based programs grow and it becomes harder to ignore the results of honest work done at high intensities, the media are taking notice. They now periodically feature health-related stories on the benefits of weight training versus aerobics-only programs, and boot-camp-type classes are now available at YMCAs all over the country, thus exposing more women to the idea that maybe harder does in fact work better.

The interesting thing is that everybody really already knows this, because there are few examples in life that don't follow the basic rules of the universe, the ones that dictate the behavior of everything. One of the most basic of those rules is that, with the exception of the occasional lottery winner, you pretty much get out of an effort what you put into it. We're all quite familiar with this reality, although we are often willing to believe people who tell us otherwise, about exercise and about life. The sooner everybody – *both* halves of the population – accepts the fact that effective exercise is more like training for athletics and less like lying around on the floor, more about performance and less about appearance, the sooner it will be understood that women really don't need their own figure salon.

Strong Enough?

"Quotation, n: The act of repeating erroneously the words of another."

Ambrose Pierce

"So far as I can remember, there is not one word in the Gospels in praise of intelligence."

Bertrand Russell

Training for the Aged

I am very old. At this writing I'm 51, and in the grand scheme of things that's not very old, I know. But yesterday I did a relatively intense deadlift workout, and I feel more like 71 just sitting here typing, and about 81 when I stand up to get coffee. This is in stark contrast to my previous existence as a young man, one who could have done the workout I did last night as back-off sets after the actual training. This is because I have accumulated lots of injuries, I don't sleep well, and – since I don't sleep well, or possibly as a cause of not sleeping well – I don't recover very fast. This affects my training schedule, my "progress," and my very purpose for training. In short, I am a masters lifter, and maybe you are too. Or maybe you will be, if you're as boneheaded, tenacious, and afraid as I am.

Masters lifters are obviously different from their younger hard-training counterparts. We have accumulated injuries that have to be considered when training is programmed. And more importantly, our response to training is blunted by our age: the stress/adaptation relationship is a function of the hormonal milieu, and old guys have an old-guys milieu.

I am literally afraid to quit training. It is tempting sometimes, like right now, to settle in to a routine that doesn't make me hurt one way or another most of the time. But I have had some limited experience with layoffs, and I don't do well without training, physically or psychologically. After even a couple of weeks my back starts to hurt in the absence of some type of work; it has apparently adapted to the abuse, as a heroin addict has to the drug. My knees feel better when I squat: I actually think they keep the bone spurs ground down. I have grown fond of high-volume chin-ups, and I'm pretty sure that they are helping me stave off rotator cuff surgery.

I don't like the way I feel without the work, and I don't think I'd like the way I would feel about myself without the work. Most guys my age – the ones at my class reunion a couple of years ago, for instance – are just physical piles of crap, looking many years older than even me. I am still just vain enough that this is motivational. I am scared enough of looking like this, and feeling like this, that I did a deadlift workout last night that hurts me today, beyond the normal soreness that a younger, less-beat-up guy would experience.

So I suppose I'll continue to train until some horrible accident prevents me from be able to. I suspect that there are many others like me, because I know at least a couple personally.

Not every masters lifter is like me. The great Olympic weightlifter Fred Lowe continues to train pretty heavy and compete at the national level in open competition. Fred is smarter and better designed than I am. In powerlifting, Jim Lem squatted 600 pounds in the 181-pound weight class in the 60-64 age group in 1989 (before the modern era of squat suits that added 300 pounds to the lift). This qualifies as legitimate. Right here in Texas there are several magnificent specimens of older manhood still lifting well; Gary Deal and Bob Ward come to our meets every year, and the masters division is usually fairly busy. And all over the world there are examples of 50-year-old-plus masters athletes who compete at or close to the open division level.

But lots of masters lifters – and maybe most of us – train hurt. It's either that or not train at all, so we train hurt. WFAC's very own Phil Anderson is having both his knees replaced in six weeks and swears he's going to squat 405 *this* week, and I promise you the silly bastard will do it. (He got 385 and missed 405. *Ed.)* This kind of thing is why he's having his knees replaced, and probably most of us think like him: so what if it hurts? We've been training so long that the idea of not training is worse than the reality of hurting. No, this is not especially intelligent, but it is the way we think.

This attitude does not lend itself well to sympathy for people who claim that "pain" prevents them from exercising. I have Phil's knee x-ray and my lumbar MRI up on the wall here; they are ugly. I'll bet you that the vast majority of people who claim a diagnosis of "fibromyalgia" (which is really a description of symptoms, not a diagnosis) are not retired powerlifters who still train.

Accumulating injuries are the price we pay for the thrill of not having sat around on our asses. It is common knowledge that training prevents injuries, arthritis, loss of bone density, and a bunch of that other fun stuff that often happens as people age. That's not what I mean here. Training hard for competitive athletics and living hard for whatever reason has the potential to hurt you, and it usually does. For me, motorcycle wrecks, horse wrecks, barbell wrecks, and overuse injuries have produced changes that alter the way I train (and live), and that must be figured in to any training plans I make. If I wrote them all down here, it would sound like I was whining, and we can't have that. Everybody my age that's been active and had any fun will have their own story. Injuries to knees, backs, elbows, wrists, and necks can all produce program-altering changes in the ability to perform key elements of barbell-based training, and often they restrict the progress possible because of the resulting mechanical inability to squat, press, or pull from the floor.

Knees take a beating from most activities that involve rapid changes in direction. Most sports available to recreational athletes – softball, volleyball, and most commonly and worst of all, soccer, the most dangerous sport in the world – carry a risk of knee injury. Neck and back injuries are often work-related, and are avoidable only through the constant mindfulness of load handling skills; they affect a huge percentage of the population. Wrist and elbow injuries are less common, especially for non-athletes, and often of an overuse nature, and some are actually preventable with exercise, like carpal tunnel syndrome. Some are not; tennis elbow is thought by some to be a permanent condition once it is established, correctable only be surgery. Car wrecks are a common feature of modern existence, and can radically alter the function of the body and the course of a life. The lasting effects of such accidents must be dealt with, and training with them is perhaps the single best way.

Chronic injuries also tend to screw up the hormonal milieu by causing the production of excessive levels of cortisol. Injuries always involve inflammation, because healing involves the repair of injured tissue and inflammation is a part of that process. Cortisol is a hormone secreted by the adrenal cortex, perched on top of the kidneys. Among its other functions, it acts as a *catabolic,* or "tearing-down" (as opposed to *anabolic,* or "building-up") hormone. Its catabolic function is – at the right point in the process – to tear down inflamed tissue to help it heal, and in this way it acts as an anti-inflammatory. But large amounts of inflammation, as might be experienced with continually aggravated chronic injuries and new acute injuries, can cause larger-than-normal amounts of cortisol to be released, causing problems with its other functions – insulin antagonism, immune system regulation, electrolyte balance, and the regulation of various other hormones and neurotransmitters – as well as turning loose its catabolic capacity on healthy tissue. Injuries must be managed carefully for this reason, but training hard enough to force progress and light enough to keep injuries at bay is a tough juggle.

But progress is possible, and the amount of progress that can be made is a function of where you are in your training progression. There are many, many examples of fine competitive athletes who started their careers later in life. And if you start lifting when you're 55, you're still a novice, just like the kid who starts when he's 18.

You won't have the same progress trajectory as the kid; you have just as far to go to reach your genetic potential, but you won't get there as fast—if you have the time, the dedication, and the desire to get there at all. Both of you have to pay the same attention to programming variables and lifestyle choices (nutrition, sleep, recovery, etc.), and both of you will go through the same stages of advancement as those variables are controlled to produce an adaptation to the stress of training. But masters lifters have a blunted response to physical stress due to the sad, rotten, unfortunate, and irritating fact that we have far lower levels of the anabolic hormones that aid in recovery and adaptation. And this, as much as your list of injuries, has the potential to limit your progress.

As we age, men rapidly lose the advantage we have over women when we are younger. Testosterone levels peak in our mid-twenties, hold relatively steady for another decade, and then begin to fall like women's clothes at the parties we don't get invited to any more. By the time we're in our late forties, lots of guys are quite literally running on hormonal fumes. This is not good because, if you think about it, we are really not designed to *be* in our late forties; when human physiology was developing a couple of million years ago, nobody lived to be any older than about 25, and the unforeseen consequences of the artificially-enhanced longevity provided by society had no way to get planned for, what with hyenas eating everybody so careless as to get to 26. These same friendly hyenas rendered Cave Guy free of concern for Alzheimer's, melanoma, prostate cancer, and the need for reading glasses.

Growth hormone drops off the same way, and it is less sexist about it. As we age, both men and women lose the ability to produce GH in response to stimuli that would normally cause an increase in its level in a younger organism. Growth hormone aids in recovery by stimulating the secretion of insulin-like growth factor I (IGF-I), the stuff that actually causes repair and recovery to occur. GH secretion declines with advancing age, and there is a linear relationship between GH and IGF-I levels, and therefore a linear relationship between age and the ability to recover from heavy work. Since they are always blessed with low testosterone levels, women primarily rely on GH for their endocrine response to training, which leads us to the rather inescapable conclusion that the older men get, the more like older women we become, hormonally speaking.

The reduction in level with age of both of these hormones is, of course, totally and completely a function of the histology of the tissues secreting the hormone, since 1) humans did not live long enough to develop a physiology adapted to low levels of anabolic hormones, 2) significant aging always takes place after reproduction and therefore has no bearing on human evolution, and, even if it did, 3) there is no adaptive advantage to be obtained from losing the ability to recover efficiently from heavy work. The human body does not intentionally lose the ability to secrete the hormones it needs to recover; it's just one o' them rotten deals, the effects of an aging endocrine system.

Weight training helps in that it keeps the hormone stimulus/response system functioning much better – and deteriorating much less slowly – than that of an aging sedentary person. Both testosterone and growth hormone secretion are pulsitile and diurnal, meaning that they vary in amount and level during the course of the day. They also vary in response to stress; a manageable, beneficial stress event like a workout causes a short-term increase in good hormone levels. Training maintains higher total average hormone levels, greater sensitivity to those levels, and the continued ability to produce an increase in response to stress.

But it's still not the rosy scenario we'd like it to be. Many things can contribute to a less-than-perfect anabolic response to training in the masters division. The main problem is that we generally don't sleep as well at 50 as we did at 18. This is because 18-year-old kids don't know what a mortgage is, have never really worried about their hemorrhoids, haven't been in a significant argument with a taxing authority, have never unwillingly slept on the couch, do not react that badly to isolated instances of excessive alcohol consumption, have not gotten subpoenas, never sunburn their bald spots, do not refer to ibuprofen as "Vitamin I," and very seldom wake up twice in the middle of the night to pee and then have trouble falling back asleep because they are worrying about remembering to change the oil in the car. Between those stressors themselves and the sleep disruptions they induce, we're in for a double shot of cortisol cocktail.

Sleep is critical to recovery. Nighttime sleep is the period during which hormone levels peak. Theoretically, at least. If the cycle is repeatedly interrupted, if it never achieves the level of depth that supports good levels of hormone production, or if it takes place during the daylight hours, the hormone response is less than optimal. A younger person is making enough testosterone and GH that their infrequent sleep abnormalities are not terribly significant, but for an older lifter bad sleep is like a shingles outbreak on a broken leg. We're not making enough anyway, and bad sleep disrupts the production of the tiny little bit we have left.

So when an older person starts a training program, their ability to progress is affected by these factors, and a different set of expectations should be anticipated. Take for example the case of a 50-year-old soccer player who decides he's had enough of running around in silly-looking shorts and hurting his knees and now wants to train for strength and *Be Somebody*. This guy will make rapid initial progress just like a younger guy, but not as much, not as fast, and not for as long a period before he slows down. On a graph the curve of his novice period of linear increase will have the same general shape as that of the younger athlete, but it will flatten out faster and at a lower position on the graph. His progress will be linear in that he can add weight to every workout, but the increases will have to be smaller if he is not to get stuck quickly. And his injuries may prevent the use of important exercises: if his knee cartilage is too screwed up to squat, this will have a profound effect on his progress since he will be unable to use the best exercise in existence for producing quantifiable, controllable, useful stress and adaptation. He will have to use more complicated, complex training programming much sooner than a younger lifter would, because he will exhaust his ability to rapidly adapt to linear increases in stress much more quickly than a kid with a more cooperative endocrine system and no chronic injuries.

A 40-year-old mother of two active teenage girls who decides she's had enough of merely wanting to look and feel like she did when she was 25 might choose to start a program with competitive overtones. She will immediately look, feel, and perform better, but not at the same rapid pace her kids would experience, assuming they had a decent coach. Under expert guidance and with grim determination, she can actually obtain the same fitness level as her kids, but in a year rather than six months. And with a couple more decades of the kind of experience provided only by life, she has the benefit of actually appreciating what she accomplishes.

It is likely that most people who start training later in life do it more for personal reasons than for the possibility of a professional sports career or a college scholarship. For this reason, most masters lifters will never need programming any more complex than that used by intermediate-level athletes. Some of us, like me and Phil, have long since left behind any possibility of lifting the weights we did twenty years ago. Personal records are reserved for brand-new exercises we either have never done before or have just invented. We are training to stave off death and further decrepitude, not to win competitions. As such, we are way out on the far right-side of the curve, the area of the graph that approaches the x-axis again. It's not as much fun as placing well in a meet you've trained hard for, but it is more fun that using a walker.

Masters lifters should follow a few common-sense rules, if they can stand it:

- Know where you are in your training progression, and try to act like it is important to you. If you are just starting out, aim for steady, constant progress every workout. If you are a retired competitor, resist the temptation to try to do things you think you "ought" to be able to do. Be realistic about this and things will go better.
- If you're an older novice, you're not going to grow as fast as a younger person, and if you are a retired competitor, you sure as hell aren't going to grow as fast as you used to. Don't eat like you are. This is how people who are actually in pretty good shape get to look like they're not.
- Don't be afraid to take a day, a week, or a month off if you think you need to. It won't kill you, but not doing so just might.
- Approach new exercises with respect. When adding a new movement to your program, don't *ever* go as heavy as you can the first time. Aim for about half of

138

what you think you can do, and the second time go about 75 percent, saving the heavy effort for the third time or beyond. This may be the best advice in this whole sorry article. Please heed it.

- Listen to your body. That is cliché, but things get to be clichés for a reason. If your elbow is pissed off, don't blame it—blame you, and don't just go ahead and press heavy anyway. This will be the most ignored advice in this article.
- Training is supposed to be fun, at least most of the time. If it stops being fun, maybe you are doing something wrong. This is also not training's fault, it's yours. Take a short layoff and then change something.

Older athletes are some of our better people. They are responsible, structured, brave individuals with a strong work ethic and great intelligence, determination, and character, and we need more of them. Yes, more people like me and Phil. Save your Advil coupons for us.

Strong Enough?

Phil, back in The Day.

Silly Bullshit

I have been accused of being an asshole on more than one occasion. This is probably due to the fact that I am an asshole, and compounded by the additional fact that I speak my mind rather too easily. I tell you this to provide context for the following remarks, some of which may cause people less cynical than me to take exception. But here we go.

There is a lot of advice, information, and well understood knowledge regarding the field in which I practice – strength training and fitness – that is just silly bullshit. Plain old "SB" (to keep from baiting the censors too temptingly). And it comes from numerous sources: chief among them are medical professionals who think that they are also exercise professionals, muscle magazines published specifically for the purpose of perpetuating it, home exercise and weight loss advertisers, internet fitness sites, the academic exercise people, and the mainstream media, who are the mindless pawns of the others.

Let's start with medical professionals who practice more than merely medicine. Doctors who treat exercise as a subset of orthopedics or cardiology are more common than those who regard it as a separate discipline that merits *actual study*. These folks are sufficiently arrogant about the vast scope of their knowledge that they probably will offer to fix your television if you mention that it broke while you're at their office for your tendinitis.

Here's an example of exercise advice from a doctor who doesn't understand a few key points. From the website of Gabe Mirkin, M.D., we receive the following wisdom: *"Exercise does not make you stronger. If it did, marathon runners would have the largest muscles of all athletes."* (This reflects the common conception in the medical community that long slow distance equals exercise.) *"The single stimulus to make muscles larger and stronger is to stretch them while they contract."* (Since this is obviously impossible, I assume he means an eccentric phase.) *"When you try to lift a heavy weight, your muscles stretch before the weight starts to move."* (Yep, he means eccentric.) *"The greater the stretch, the greater the damage to the muscle fibers and when they heal after a few days, the greater the gain in strength. The results for this study give a clear message. You become stronger by lifting heavier weights, not by exercising more."*

Fascinating. His last sentence is correct, but if I am correctly interpreting his poorly informed comments – and I believe I am – he apparently thinks that no one gets stronger without an eccentric phase included in their chosen exercise. Power snatches, power cleans, and throwing heavy things cannot make you strong. Yet look at this from another article on strength for cycling: *"Competitive cyclists gain tremendous leg muscle strength just by climbing steep hills very fast, which exerts as much force on their leg muscles as weightlifting and makes them very strong."*

The man doesn't understand that riding a bike completely lacks an eccentric component, but he claims that you can still get strong by climbing hills. And here is a repeated theme: *"All athletic training is done by stressing your muscles with a hard workout, taking easy workouts until the soreness disappears, and then taking another hard workout."* The notion that training while sore is detrimental appears in many articles on his website, and reflects a lack of understanding of how advanced athletes train and adapt to their training.

This is typical of the level of understanding that physicians bring to the weight room. The recommendation to wait until soreness is gone to train again indicates a complete lack of practical experience with weight training, experience that would teach the necessity of training while sore for virtually every athlete who wants to improve. And the failure to understand the difference between eccentric and concentric types of contractions is understandable in a lay person, but not for a *doctor with a fitness website.*

And isn't it fascinating that your pediatrician will always advise you to prevent your child from lifting weights, an activity that in any incarnation is far safer than most other things kids can do, but will never, ever advise against soccer – the most dangerous sport in the world. (Go ahead, Dr. Sultemeier, look it up. I dare you.)

We have doctors to thank for lots of SB. The advice to always ask a doctor before you (yes, *you*) start any exercise program is rather self-serving, considering the fact that they are the ones billing for the office visit, and the silliness of insisting that a healthy 35-year-old get a checkup before he starts to lift weights makes one suspicious of the actual purpose. As mentioned earlier, the medical community is famous for equating exercise with running, walking, cycling, and other such monostructural aerobic-pathway activities that are measured by the time spent engaging in them. The pamphlet rack in the waiting room is typically stuffed completely full of references to "20 minutes of exercise a day, 5 days a week," as if the only way to quantify a stress that leads to an adaptation is with your Polar RS 800 fancy watch/heart rate monitor.

Strong Enough?

Tommy Suggs, my old lifting friend, once said, "If I had to choose between looking like a marathon runner or having a heart attack, I'd take the heart attack." How running 26.2 miles at one time ever got to be associated with a Good Thing just beats the absolute hell out of me. Yet it is held up to everybody as the *sine qua non* of physical accomplishment. Why, the very term "sports medicine" actually means "treatment of running-induced overuse injuries." Long slow distance training – or LSD, as it has come to be called – is not only a poor way to lose bodyfat and gain cardiovascular fitness; it may be the single best way (especially when combined with the FDA's dietary recommendations) to lose muscle mass ever devised, and it has never made anyone stronger (as even Dr. Mirkin knows). Yet the vast majority of exercise advice from the medical community involves LSD of one type or another: the old traditional workhorse of the LSD world, jogging, its even more ineffective little brother, walking, or their still less effective but more fun and better-looking cousin, cycling. All these activities can be measured in minutes, which makes them easy to prescribe but also renders the prescription virtually meaningless, as it completely ignores the intensity at which the exercise is done. The "S" is usually overemphasized by people doing LSD.

This little tidbit is one of the problems with most advice from medical types. Their idea of exercise is so conservative that it fails to produce enough stress to force an adaptation. LSD is not sufficiently consumptive of oxygen and substrate to cause an actual improvement in aerobic capacity; people get better at moving their feet and pumping and oxygenating blood, but only within the limited context of the easy, infinitely repeatable, short range of motion, low-force non-stress provided by an activity like walking or jogging a 15-minute mile. An actual improvement in VO_2 max is stimulated only by an effort intense enough to depress O_2 saturation, and that requires more stress than CYA exercise prescriptions are willing to advise. And their model of strength training is just funny as hell. The American College of Sports Medicine recommends – for all who consider themselves apparently healthy and adult – eight to ten exercises using a minimum of one set (but maybe as many as three if you are *really serious*) of eight to twelve repetitions (ten to fifteen if you are frail, in which case you apparently need more endurance work and less strength so that you can continue to effectively maintain your frail status) to the point of volitional fatigue, two to three days per week in a slow and controlled manner through a "full range of motion." In other words, the ACSM wants you to do Nautilus training. But not too hard. And never, ever hold your breath, lest you join the pile of corpses on the floor of my gym that performed the Valsalva maneuver during a heavy set of five squats.

This overly conservative approach to strength training is derived from the version – the only version – of "exercise" that is taught in medical and physical therapy school: rehabilitation. The training of doctors, physical therapists, and athletic trainers requires no formal education in strength training, especially not the effective, barbell kind of strength training used by athletes who are serious about improving their performance. They are taught a method for getting sick and injured people back to "normal parameters," not how to take a healthy athlete from baseline to elite athletics, or even how to make a healthy non-athlete fitter and stronger. Their unwillingness to recognize the difference is the problem they don't know they've got.

On the other hand, the folks who publish muscle magazines ought to know better when it comes to legitimate information about strength and conditioning. And they actually do, since significant numbers of them used to be athletes or bodybuilders. They just don't care. (Or, more likely, care more about the quantity in their wallets than the quality in their pages.) Over the past four decades, the fitness media has developed (*evolved* is the wrong word) from some fairly informative monthly publications (Peary Rader's *Iron Man*, Joe Weider's *Muscle*, Bob Hoffman's *Strength and Health*) and a handful of newsletters to a landslide of monthly misinformation primarily intended to sell supplements and other advertising. The July 2007 issue of *Flex* is 56 percent ad copy (179 of 320 pages), and one of the articles is six pages about whey protein. The other articles are all the same, the photography is all the same, and the emphasis is on appearance, not performance.

Muscle and fitness magazines are also largely responsible for giving women who desperately need to build some muscle mass the only excuse they'll ever need to remain flabby: the certain knowledge that if they lift weights they'll get "big, bulky muscles," just like Ronnie Coleman and me. They are terribly careless when they prominently feature pictures of female physique competitors who are all too apparently willing to do enough steroids to grow huge muscles – the very kind that ladies are afraid of – without a disclaimer to that effect. The overwhelming majority of the female population is not capable of building huge, masculine muscles, or noses, chins, ears, hands, veins, feet, beards, eyebrows, and all the other little details that separate the boys from the girls. Pictures of females who have taken this rather drastic step in a rather atypical direction should not be viewed by impressionable housewives trying to decide whether to start a weight training program. It's bad for membership sales, and I have to think it can't be terribly good for supplement sales either. Yet the publishers seem to be oblivious to the fact that they have created an objection to be overcome every time an uninformed woman comes into a place that offers more than Pilates, yoga, and treadmills.

And muscle magazines are at least partly to blame for an epidemic of SB concerning teenage boys and young men. A recent trend has developed amongst these little snots that makes it very difficult to put any muscular bodyweight on them: they all seem to think they have to have visible abs, even if it means staying at a bodyweight of 135 pounds. They all want a "six-pack" despite the fact that they don't have an ice chest to put it in. They won't eat breakfast, they eat some type of fast food goo for lunch, and if they eat supper it's because Mom made them. This is intentional, and is their version of "dieting" to keep that trim, fit look.

Now don't misunderstand my concern here: I know that we live in a society largely dominated by fat slobs. Maybe not where you live, but where I live this is true, and I suspect that the vast majority of the United States suffers this unintended result of our economic prosperity. So any drift in the opposite direction is fine, right? Look, when high school and college-age kids come to me and ask how to put on muscle and I take the time to tell them and then they won't do it because they're afraid they'll lose their Washboard Abs, it pisses me off to waste my time with people who ask and then won't listen to what I *know* will work for what they *claim* to be trying to do, and, well, it just gets *aggravating*, you know? And it's all because they actually think that 1) if they have abs they'll look like Ronnie Coleman and me, 2) chicks really dig a six-pack, and 3) what does Rip know anyway?

Well, Rip knows that a 135-pound 5' 9" 18-year-old kid doesn't look like either Ronnie or Rip, even if he has a twelve-pack, and that if he seriously wants to head in that direction the first thing to do is to gain about 60 pounds. Ole Rip also knows that women don't really care about abs – they care about Other Things. And after all, you asked Rip; he didn't ask you. So put down your *Muscle and Fiction*, do your squats, drink your milk, and pay better attention to the answers when you ask the questions.

Next on the agenda are infomercials: the symptom of a healthy economy and a failing public education system, and the primary purveyor of SB in the modern world. This very second, a 30-minute TV program is in progress that is predicated on the assumption that you are stupid. Depending on which one you watch, you will be told that sitting in a little rotating chair will give you six-pack abs, that juicing all your vegetables will give you six-pack abs, that jumping rope/dancing to very specific types of music/pretending to kickbox/turbojamming (all of which feature things called "moves") will give you six-pack abs. You might be encouraged to buy an Ab Roller, Ab Lounger, Ab Belt, Ab Energizer, AbTronic, Ab Rocker, Ab Doer, Ab Force, Ab Swing, Ab Rocket, Ab Flex, Ab Dolly, Ab Away Pro, Ab Lifter Plus, Abrageous, FastAbs, HipHop Abs, or 6-Second Abs by the promise that they will give you six-pack abs. The iGallop really looks like fun – Like riding a horse! – and will give you six-pack abs. You might even own a ThighMaster, bought many years ago (Still available today! Call now!) because they promised that it would give you six-pack abs.

Yes, there is a definite pattern here. Cheesy appeals to everyone's desire for the chiseled midsection – which really comes only from hard work, eating correctly, and, in some cases, genetic predisposition – shamelessly offer results to people not willing to pay anything more than money for them. It is always easy, it is always fast, and for some reason it is always *abs*. Even Chuck Norris's Total Gym gizmo, which claims to be better than free weights, dwells on abs, although, in fairness, not quite as much as everything else does.

These devices always promise to take fat off of your belly. Apparently *just* your belly. Spot reduction – the idea that somehow fat soaks out of your adipose tissue and straight into the muscles you're working right now, or the equally weird idea that fat is loosened in a specific place by some device or a certain aspect of an exercise, travels straight to the kidneys, and is then "flushed out," despite the fact that no one's ever seen any floating in the place it supposedly gets flushed into – is as integral to weight-loss popular culture as Richard Simmons. Spot reduction is really stupid, but I'd be surprised if 95 percent of the population doesn't accept it as fact, because they want to believe so very badly. It's like you were about Santa Claus when you were nine.

And that's just the stuff that promises miracles with some special kind of "exercise." There are pills on the market that cut right to the chase: lose fat with no work *at all*. None. Cortislim, Zantrex-3, Leptoprin, Propolene, Relacore, Tetrazene, and lots and lots of other products promise effort-free weight loss with various blends of stimulant herbs. It is astonishingly apparent that if there were any pill, any medication, available anywhere that actually worked, there would be only about three fat people in North America. Because aside from those three people who keep showing up on *Oprah* encouraging us to accept them, everybody else wants to be fit and slim, and a pill fits what they're willing to do to get there just about perfectly.

Internet "fitness" sites, of course, are not exempt from this tirade. In addition to websites of the type operated by the aforementioned Dr. Mirkin, there are many shining examples. Here is an excerpt from one of my favorite websites, www.womensportsnutrition.com:

> *The skin is the largest organ in and around your body. The skin makes up approximately 80-90% of your body weight and personality. Your skin has trillions of cells which are being replaced every second by the millions. This replacement enables you to keep your youthful look and prevent the aging process. Each cell is made up of memory, intelligence, and energy governed by the nutritional chemistry of DNA and RNA. This, along with hemoglobin, the nutritional part of your blood that makes skin glow, makes up the chemistry that keeps your original, youthful design and separate male and female personality features and characteristics.*

Now, I am not clever enough to make up this particularly high grade of SB. It is the work of one Donna F. Smith, C.C.N., C.N. If you happen to live in the greater Wichita Falls area, you could visit her sometime for a Clinical and Sports Nutrition Comprehensive Analysis (CSNCA), $195, a Comprehensive Health Appraisal (HAC),

$45, or a Deferred Re-Evaluation Analysis (DRA), a bargain at only $250. What do you suppose somebody who thinks the skin makes up 90 percent of your body weight will tell you about nutrition? (Of course, she says that the skin makes up 90 percent of your personality too, so social interaction with her may be awkward.) The traditional medical community, whose authority "Dr." Smith desperately wants to invoke, has no stranglehold on the supply of SB.

If the mainstream media are good at anything it is the mindless dissemination of hearsay and innuendo. The hairdos of the networks, hairdo-wannabes that work for the TV stations at the local level, the journalism majors who write for the smaller newspapers, and the grown-up journalism majors who write for the big newspapers and wire services are prominent, prolific sources of SB. These people regularly mangle information from everyone else's specialty too, so we strength and fitness folks need not feel singled out. (The enormity of this topic is beyond the scope of this humble venue, but we'll discuss it over beer sometime soon, just you and me.) Few of the news reports on recently published scientific studies preserve much of the detail of the actual paper, certainly not enough to sort through the generalization errors made by the newsreader hired for his rugged good looks reading gibberish that attempts to summarize a twelve-page paper in four sentences for a lay audience. What starts out as "Peak Power, Ground Reaction Forces, and Velocity During the Squat Exercise Performed at Different Loads" becomes "A recent study finds that exercises with heavier weights should be done at slower speeds. The findings, by Dr. Attila Zink of the University of Miami, Coral Gables, reported this week, determine that the heavier a weight being lifted is, the slower it will move, and the lighter a weight is, the faster it can move." Or, possibly, "A recent study has determined that full squats are bad for your knees." And if you think the news report is SB, you should read the paper: a classic case of garbage in/SB out.

Which brings up another good point: the academic exercise community cannot seem to understand that poorly designed studies, such as the one above, are not helpful, and in fact add to the general level of SB that gets accepted as Truth. They cannot even see that the studies are poorly designed. The study cited above, for example, was supposed to measure the effects of "squats" on vertical jump performance when done in immediate proximity to the test. The squats they tested were "half squats" and "quarter squats." First, I have no problem with using partial squats in a testing protocol if that's what these guys want to do, but they don't even quantify the movements; they just say that they are "demonstrated in Figures 1 and 2, respectively." Figure 1 shows a kid with his knees and hips at somewhere between 95 and 105 degrees, and Figure 2 shows the kid with his knees and hips just barely unlocked; no depth markers, no angles measured, no anything measured, just pictures. This, my friends, is not science. It is guesswork. It might be useful for other scientists to able to reproduce this experiment in case the findings turned out to be unusual, controversial, or otherwise important (they didn't), but without actual standards for the tests used, this would be impossible (even if they did). And secondly and most incredibly, they *actually tested a half squat and quarter squat one-rep max!* I am overwhelmed by the silliness of such a thing. Anybody who has ever trained with weights, who has ever done squats, and who has ever had any personal experience with heavy weights on their back whatsoever knows that you can quarter-squat just about whatever you can load on the bar, because a quarter squat is whatever you want it to be. Five degrees of angle might be worth another 50 pounds, so it matters how deep your quarter squats and half squats are done. It therefore really doesn't matter what the conclusion of the study was; it is SB by definition.

Sadly, this is the quality of a vast amount of the exercise science literature. A high percentage of the published studies have a glaring methodology flaw that renders the results meaningless, or at least suspect. And the reason is that the folks doing the research lack sufficient personal experience with the subject being investigated to understand that they are generating SB. Quarter squats may look good on paper, but unless you have personally taken pride in telling your buddies that you squatted 750—when in reality you quarter-squatted 750 and can only actually squat 395— you don't really have a handle on why your study is SB.

For example, the recent the fad in exercise is "core stability", which is apparently obtained by rolling around on inflated rubber balls and doing very light asymmetrical exercises from a position of unbalance. It sounds scientific, it looks complicated, and it would never have occurred to you, so it must be valuable, right? No. It is classic SB. A heavy overhead squat produces core stability. So does a heavy back squat, especially if you remain stable while you do it. I don't care how hard it is to stay on a wobble board for 30 minutes; it doesn't accomplish anything either quantifiable or significant outside the context of injury rehab, and any type of squats work better. And if you haven't ever done heavy squats, you lack the experience to understand why this is true. Many academics and most physical therapists haven't.

Strong Enough?

What is it that drives the dissemination of silly bullshit? The drive comes from commercial interest (obviously) and ego (amazing!). Donna Smith could use the money; so can I, so I appreciate this motivation. The magazine people want you to keep buying them, and to buy from their advertisers, and if they make sure to hire writers that have "CSCS" beside their names, they have covered their asses. The fine folks who bring you HipHop Abs, the Ab Roller, and Cortislim are counting on the fact that you will probably fail to do your homework. On the other hand, Dr. Mirkin probably isn't in a jam for the cash, so he just likes the idea of being a Fitness Expert in addition to a doctor (and, for all I know, maybe a very good one in his actual field of specialty). The orthopod who tells you that full squats are bad for the knees and they'll stunt your growth, and that you need to just do lighter weights and use higher reps because "they do the same thing," doesn't expect you to pay him for this advice; he's throwing it in for free. He knows he's qualified because after all he *is* a doctor. The exercise science people have qualified themselves. And the media don't care who's qualified; they just need a story to fill 45 seconds.

The problem is complex, and the solution is simple. It is incumbent on you, yes You, to educate yourself to a sufficient extent that you are in a position to evaluate information issued from a position of authority. You are supposed to be able to recognize silly bullshit when you hear it. And I'm sorry if it's hard to have to think all the time, but the consequences of placing your responsibility to do so in the hands of others can result in a closet full of Thigh Masters, which will make it necessary to find somewhere else to hang your shirts—like on your Bowflex.

Strong Enough?

"There is nothing worse than aggressive stupidity."

Johann Wolfgang von Goethe

"When you discover you are riding a dead horse, the best strategy is to dismount. But other strategies with dead horses [include] the following: buying a stronger whip; changing riders; saying things like "this is the way we've always ridden this horse"; ... and, finally, harnessing several dead horses together for increased speed."

Judge Thomas Penfield Jackson

Strong Enough?

It's been a hard year here at Wichita Falls Athletic Club. We've lost a couple of very worthwhile folks since last summer, and another good friend of mine died recently. Cardell was 45 when he was diagnosed with an ascending aortic aneurism that possibly involved the aortic valve. He was prepared for a complicated, dangerous operation, but sepsis developed almost immediately after the surgery, and he died as a result of complications from the infection. The reason I mention this rather unhappy personal item is that it took him three and a half weeks to die. That's a long time in the ICU, and he lasted that long because he was very, very strong. Cardell completely ruptured his patellar tendon at work a couple of years ago, a devastating injury that could easily have left him crippled for life. But he was strong, and five months after the surgery he squatted 315 pounds for 5 reps to our standards here at WFAC. Strong people are harder to kill than weak people, and more useful in general.

Strength is the ability to produce force, and it is possibly the most important component in athletics. It is dependent on muscle mass, on the nerves that make the muscles fire, and on the will that fires the nerves. Power depends on it, as does balance, coordination, speed, quickness, and endurance. Athletes will risk censure and suspension to get it; there are no steroids for improving "technique." And once they have it, they are much harder to beat: all other things being equal, the stronger athlete will always win.

Strong Enough?

Technical ability is the capacity to execute a movement efficiently – completing the movement while using the least possible energy. It is the ability to adhere very closely to an efficient motor pathway in a consistent manner. As such, it can also be defined as the ability to demonstrate the strength available to complete a given athletic task, since in its absence even great strength cannot be displayed in that movement. In this sense, strength is dependent on technical ability, even though strength is the quantity we most often seek to measure: the shot is *thrown* for distance, the bar is *lifted* for the most weight, the ball is *hit* over the fence, the lineman *tackles* the fullback hard enough to stop him. These are more obvious examples of strength display, but all sports worthy of the name depend on force production within the context of correct technical execution.

Yet there are a number of competitive sports with athletes and coaches who think strength is not a terribly critical component of performance. Sports like swimming, fencing, cycling, soccer, cricket, tennis, boxing, and hockey pay lip service at some minimal level to strength training, but it is not a major part of most athletes' preparation for competition in those sports, and barbells are not a significant component of what little strength work there is. Even rugby, with its reputation as a big man's sport, has no organized school of thought on how to incorporate strength training. There will be isolated examples of individual athletes who utilize strength training to a greater extent than their peers, of course, and these people will usually be dominant in their sport – in part because of the training, and in part because of the motivation level of an athlete who actively seeks to prepare for excellence outside the normal realm of training and outside the actual field of play.

Strong Enough?

The amazing thing is that the sport of weightlifting is one of these. There is a school of thought – in the United States especially – that holds that training for correct technique in the snatch and the clean and jerk is more important than training for strength. Now that I've brought it up, the guilty will deny it. But I know what is being done to train our country's weightlifters at the highest levels – lots of us know – and it's not what you would call strength training. Athletes who go for extended periods of time without being asked to do a PR back squat or press, or any kind of heavy deadlift at all, are not being trained for strength in the usual sense of the term. And if you are one of those folks who are prone to dismiss anyone not directly involved with the National Program as not entitled to an opinion, you might as well stop right here. My opinion can be evaluated independently of my credentials, and if you are capable of doing that, you have my permission to continue reading.

The case against a major role for strength training in technique-dependent sports is not always stated this way exactly. It may be claimed that time spent getting strong could be more productively spent improving technique; I think this is true only for athletes with bad technique. It also depends on the nature of the sport, as we'll see later. Or it may be claimed that technique contributes more to performance than strength, which might be true for golf and a few other games and activities but is not true for athletics. A golf club's business end is not very heavy, and the accuracy with which it is directed is much more critical than the small amount of force necessary to accelerate it around the body during the swing. (As an aside, Gary Player just announced that At Least One Pro Golfer That He Knows Of has taken steroids, and that random drug testing must begin immediately in the PGA to stave off the decay that now haunts Major League Baseball. This renders me astonished, puzzled, and amused. A large number of PGA professionals who win lots of money are fat chain-smokers. There is even a local golfer here in Wichita Falls who shoots in the 70s and will damn sure take your money, despite the fact that he is 72, smokes, drinks more than I do, and has a prosthetic leg. What in the hell are these other guys wasting money on steroids for? I suspect that it has nothing to do with the actual game of golf.)

The case for strength training is a simple one. Both strength and technical ability are developable quantities that respond to a correctly designed program to make them improve. We refer to strength work as "training" and technique work as "practice." Both produce improvement in roughly the same way: easy at first, harder as you get better, and after you're really good, more improvement becomes more and more difficult – then finally impossible – to obtain. It is said to approach a "limit," a point past which further improvement cannot occur. A limit is the result of the fact that nothing can continue to improve infinitely or indefinitely. That's why new world records are not set daily in every sport. As a broad, probably overly-general rule, order in all systems increases only with the addition of energy, or "work"; entropy is the tendency of all systems toward disorder without the addition of work to combat all this heinous disorder, an observation derived from the second law of thermodynamics. To put it in another probably overly generalized way, there reaches a point at which the addition of an infinite amount of energy to a system results in an infinitely small increase in order. Order is what we mean when we say "improvement." And that, my friends, is just how the Universe operates.

The graphic representation of the approach to a limit is described as an "asymptote," a term from mathematics that describes the shape of the possible improvement curve as it approaches its limit. The limit of the ability to improve strength is ultimately controlled by an individual's genetics, as has been widely recognized. The closeness to which that limit is approached is determined by the ability to train in the most productive possible way, itself limited by time, resources, and motivation. Technical ability is limited as well, by the capacity to express mechanical efficiency. This ability is also controlled by the genetics governing neuromuscular efficiency, intelligence, sensory acuity, balance, and coordination; the closeness to which this limit is approached is a function of *practice* – its quality and quantity. In reality, these asymptotic curves get pretty wavy as they approach their limits, the result of injuries, forced layoffs, lapses in motivation, and all the other things that interrupt progress and keep the names of most great natural athletes from becoming household words. But if you pull back far enough to see the bigger picture, the curve approaches the limit smoothly, and then falls away as the career winds down.

All this should be fairly obvious, so the real question is this: What is the relationship between strength and its ability to be expressed through correct technique? Strength and technical ability are interdependent quantities. One does not exist without the other being present at some level. But it has been my experience as a coach that technique in weightlifting develops much faster than strength. Within six months of learning the snatch, any novice who has the potential to be a competitive weightlifter can do an essentially perfect snatch with, say, 30 kg, and two years later that same lifter will be snatching 100 kg with just about the same technique. The quantity that has continued to improve is strength, not technical ability. An argument can be made that technical ability must keep pace with strength, but technical ability on the snatch must remain at a level that allows the snatch to actually be performed, or you're not snatching, you're dropping the bar from overhead with a wide grip. As you improve your ability to snatch heavier weights , you are getting stronger with the same technical ability, so which quantity is actually improving? Both maybe, but strength certainly. In fact, the improvement in a weightlifter's snatch over a career looks quite similar to that of a powerlifter's squat, bench, or deadlift – movements that require only a small percentage of the technical skill required to perform a snatch.

A common argument is that some lifters are able to convert a very high percentage of their strength into the technical execution of the snatch and the clean and jerk, and that since this is the case, strength per se is not the limiting quantity. It seems to me that since strength and technical ability are interdependent quantities, there is a ratio between any individual's ability to produce a correct technical effort and a given level of strength. There are exceptionally "efficient" lifters, like Yuri Zakharevich, Anatoli Pisarenko, and Jeff Michaels, who can do a clean and jerk with a weight that is just short of their best front squat. The reason we remember who they are is because they are the exceptions. Most lifters need a margin of strength over and above their ability to execute technically so that the minute imperfections that are always present in even a nearly perfect snatch do not significantly affect the lifter's ability to finish the lift. No snatch is 100% mechanically perfect, and if sufficient strength is available it is possible to save what would otherwise be a miss by wrestling it back or forward or up as needed; in this way, enough strength makes perfect technique slightly less critical.

But these exceptional lifters still demonstrate the phenomenon of the ratio between a lifter's strength and his ability to demonstrate that strength in a technically demanding movement. This ratio may even change over time, as the athlete ages; a close ratio may be a feature of younger lifters more commonly, and most of the ones I know of in this situation are in fact young. It also varies with the conditions under which each type of max effort – squatting strength and snatch technique – is measured. If, for reasons of training schedule, strength is at peak and technical practice is not, the ratio will be different than it would be the week before a meet. But some lifters will always be more efficient than others, and that is a perfectly reasonable thing to expect. And since this ratio exists, the more easily improved quantity in the equation will drive up the value of the sum if it is increased. Those lifters who are able to clean a very high percentage of their deadlift are either very technically efficient, or not very strong, depending on your prejudice. Most lifters clean a lower – rather than higher – percentage of their deadlift, but either way, the ratio between strength and technical ability for an individual lifter is an identifiable quantity. And if the strength variable is increased and technical ability stays the same, the ability to display strength through technical ability increases. Do the math.

Strong Enough?

My point here is that after a certain level of technical improvement, which occurs relatively early in a lifter's training, the quantity that will always remain the most improvable is strength. This is because technical ability is primarily a neurological and neuromuscular phenomenon. It is developed through basic instruction, repetition, correction, mental modeling and imaging, more repetition and correction, and then a diminishing amount of correction as the movement gets embedded and the "feel" for correct performance becomes developed. This process, for a person actually capable of learning the movement (unfortunately, there do exist motor morons) takes a few weeks to a few months. The development of strength, on the other hand, takes years. The processes involved in building strength involve muscle, bone, connective tissue, and endocrine systems as well as the neuromuscular system, and the remodeling of these tissues takes time. Strength acquisition requires a much more profound change in physiology than that which accompanies the learning of a movement pattern, and the processes that bring about this change do their work over months and years, not just weeks.

And if technique has been worried about at the expense of strength, as it very well might have been for many American weightlifters, the potential for improvement in overall performance lies in strength improvement. Shane Hamman told me recently that he was quite sure that the lifters he had competed against at the international level were much stronger than he was. He cited the example of Hossein Reza Zadeh, the Iranian superheavyweight whom he saw do a 230-kg (506-pound) power clean at the 2004 Olympics "without bending his knees" at the catch. Shane said he never saw him squat anything much heavier than 280 kg (616 pounds) for a triple in the warm-up room, but a guy who is about to compete in weightlifting in the Olympics might not be inclined to do a PR back squat in the warm-up room at the meet just to show everybody. The 230 power clean was all Shane needed to see. He had the same impression of the other lifters in the "A" session, where the lifters expected to place high in the meet are grouped. Shane's opinion about strength is not to be ignored: he has squatted over 1000 pounds in suit and wraps, and I personally witnessed him squat 804 in a pair of lifting shoes, shorts, and a t-shirt – no belt or knee wraps – and handle the weight *explosively*, immediately followed by five standing back flips.

I know athletes who have been at the Olympic Training Center in the weightlifting program for various periods of time and never been asked for a PR back squat, front squat, or, god forbid, a deadlift the entire time they were there. This is a common feature of weightlifting training in this country, where the only lifts that are emphasized or coached for technique are the snatch and the clean and jerk. Some weightlifting coaches may tell you that they train the squat hard, but this critical exercise is approached with the "Just put the bar on your back and squat it" coaching method, the same one that has worked so brilliantly for high school football players for decades – to similar effect. It is as if they think that coaching the squat, the press, and the deadlift for technical correctness and efficiency is beneath their dignity, that technique is only important in the snatch and the clean and jerk. Some of their lifters even have perfect form on the two lifts, in the B session. The critical thing is that quite often the A-session lifters have less than perfect snatch and C&J form, but are strong enough that they can get away with it.

Strong Enough?

The lifters who regularly stomp us to death at the World Championships are probably not coached for strength either. Their programs have the luxury of high enough participation and a large enough pool of very strong lifters to choose from that strength coaching need not be a primary concern. China has 1.3 million registered lifters – they can find eight men and seven women strong enough to beat us without a lot of trouble. But not devoting a bunch of time to making their national team stronger doesn't mean that strength is not important to them. If you're on their team, you are by definition very damn strong. And if you can't stay strong on their program (amazingly enough, no one seems to have this problem since they usually squat or front squat every day), they can find someone else who can. Big, efficient programs like those run by most European, Asian, and some African countries advance enough athletes to the higher levels that the national team has plenty of strength talent to choose from, and the program itself does not have to focus on strength. It is just like the NFL, and for exactly the same reason—a huge talent pool and lots of feeder programs. USA Weightlifting, with its 3,000 members, is not. My point is that if your weightlifting team is good enough that you don't have to worry about making them stronger, that's wonderful, but if it isn't, you'd better do something about it. We don't seem to be.

And again, if strength is not important, why do we worry about steroids? An entire enforcement bureaucracy – USADA/WADA – now exists because of athletes' persistent use of drugs that are primarily taken to make them stronger, by whatever mechanism. Steroids do not make your technique better; they just make you able to handle heavier weights with your same technique. Bodybuilders don't use them to make their Double Biceps pose more fluid and precise. Cyclists don't use them to make their pedal stroke more efficient. Professional wrestlers don't take them to improve their Sleeper Hold. Baseball players already know how to hit the ball; steroids just help them hit it farther, not more precisely. Whatever the reason for taking them – improved recovery, neuromuscular efficiency, weight gain and leverage improvement, "tightness," aggression, and so on – they work because, ultimately, they make you stronger. And, clearly, stronger is important enough to these athletes to risk a career for.

Athletes and coaches in other sports share this misunderstanding. Judo is a martial art with strength and technique components that are not quite analogous to Olympic weightlifting. It takes to longer to gain technical proficiency in any martial art because of the much more extensive catalog of movements involved and the complex nature of their application. A weightlifting meet always involves three snatch attempts followed by three clean and jerk attempts; a judo match consists of the extemporaneous application of the appropriate number of many thousands of technique permutations, depending on conditions that change constantly over the length of the point. Technical ability in judo is arguably much more important and much harder to develop than it is in weightlifting.

Yet great strength trumps technical ability in judo, provided that the players are of similar bodyweight. The sport places a high premium on the use of leverage to overcome an opponent's strength, but at some point strength cannot be overcome by anyone save the most highly skilled player. Great strength allows imperfect technique to be forgiven. My friend Gant Grimes, an experienced and capable judoka, was once destroyed by an opponent named Brad Sanchez, a guy who had beaten a national champion despite having trained for only a few months. Sanchez was a 500-pound bencher, strong everywhere else too, and his strength rendered an opponent's superior technical ability irrelevant. Gant was chokeslammed by this guy, and he says there was literally *nothing* he could do about it.

Here is where the difference in the technical-ability learning curves for the two sports is critical; most weightlifters are experts at technique in a year, maybe two, whereas in a sport like judo, important improvements in technical ability can continue for decades. Depending on how much mat time you have accumulated – and how many months or years it takes to do so – it might behoove a judo player to spend at least a decent amount of time under the bar. And despite this fact, the vast majority of judo coaches resist the idea of adding barbell strength training to preparation for the sport.

As with most sports coaches who lack specific training or experience with barbells, their reluctance is understandable, the result of a perfectly reasonable desire to avoid coaching things they don't know about. Now, this has never stopped a high school football coach from telling his athletes to look up at the ceiling when they do their half-squats, but it is conceivable that a conscientious sensei who has never lifted weights might be reluctant to put a bar and plates in the dojo. What would not be understandable is that same sensei advising against learning barbells and spending 45 minutes twice a week doing them.

Strong Enough?

It is also understandable that endurance sports coaches might not have an appreciation of the contribution that strength training can make to training for long-slow-distance sports. The easiest way to understand how this works is to look at the example of cycling, where each pedal stroke represents the use of a percentage of absolute strength. If your absolute strength goes up (as it necessarily will when I take your narrow little cyclist ass into the gym and double your squat strength in six weeks), then the percentage of your absolute strength used on each pedal stroke at the same speed goes down (by about half). Or, the force you can apply to each stroke over your three-hour ride can go up. Either way, strength has contributed to pedaling endurance. And if you get your pull-up strength up too, you can more efficiently control the frame while you pedal: your pull on the bars decreases uncontrolled frame "rocking" and maximizes force directed to the pedals. That should be enough evidence for cycling coaches to appreciate the contribution of strength training to the sport, but somehow I don't think they will. Cycling coaches are among the most resistant human beings on earth when it comes to ideas involving things other than bicycles.

Strength is quite simply the quality that separates winners from losers. "All other things being equal," so the saying goes, "the stronger athlete will win every time." Old sayings are sometimes foolish, but not this particular one. Technical ability allows strength to be demonstrated more efficiently; however, having better technique does not make one stronger. Both are necessary, and both should be coached, trained for, and appreciated with equal enthusiasm. But even if we remove a particular sport from the discussion

169

and substitute "survival" as the activity we're training for, I'd take strength over technique every time. Cardell would agree. The process that has yielded us and every other living thing on this planet has an appreciation of strength, and we should too.

Cardell Hairrill

"I love deadlines. I like the whooshing sound they make as they fly by."

Douglas Adams

"Platitude: an idea (a) that is admitted to be true by everyone, and (b) that is not true."

H.L. Mencken

Good Form

I was driving home the other night, listening to the radio, and the guy filling in for Art Bell on Coast to Coast AM was talking to some other guy about Nazis, UFOs, the Kennedy Assassination, time travel, and George Bush, and how it all relates to OneWorldGovernment. This, of course, made me think about barbell training, and it occurred to me that good form on the barbell exercises should not be a matter for debate. People should not be entitled to their own opinion about it, any more than they are entitled to an opinion about the value of x in $3x - 10 = 60$, or whether the Grays pulled off the Bay of Pigs. Good form (or technique, or kinematics, or whatever you'd like to call doing it right) should depend on the logic of a dispassionate analysis of the body-and-barbell system in the motion required by the exercise, and that's about all. The exercise is chosen to work a particular movement pattern normal to the human skeleton, the bar has a certain path it most efficiently travels through space for the exercise, the skeleton must move in ways defined by its segment lengths and articulation points to enable this bar path, and the muscles must move the skeleton exactly this way. Anything that deviates from this is bad form.

Why is bad form a problem? Two reasons come to mind immediately. First, shoving joints into positions they are not designed to occupy presents potentially significant safety problems, although not of the magnitude you may have been led to believe. And second, allowing joints to assume positions they are not designed to occupy means work that should have been done by the muscles anatomically designated to move the bones in question actually got done by *other* muscles, whose proper function in efficiently performing the movement got circumvented by your inattention to detail. It really boils down to that: bad form – for people who know better – is just a willingness to do the movement the wrong way because that's the way you've been doing it. And the right way is better because eventually you can lift more weight correctly, in addition to the fact that you're less likely to get hurt.

If I had a nickel for every scary deadlift I've seen at high school powerlifting meets, I actually wouldn't have more than about five dollars in nickels because I quit going to the damn things after I'd been to just three or four of them. I do not enjoy seeing the egos of coaches take precedence over the spinal integrity of athletes. Little skinny kids trying to open with 405, when their backs are not capable of staying flat with 225. Beautiful little 15-year-old girls stuffed into squat suits, low backs rounded into complete flexion on their opening attempts. Big, potentially strong kids doing the lifts with technique that passes for legal at a meet of this type, with weights that they cannot lift correctly – that is, in a way that satisfies the rules of biomechanics that govern safety and efficiency. I witnessed high squats in spinal flexion, hitched deadlifts in spinal flexion, and coaches and referees behaving as though this was Just Fine. It is truly amazing that more kids are not hurt in activities of this type, and that in itself tells us something about the nature of healthy human bodies and the actual injury potential of barbell exercises.

Yes, it's harder to hurt people with barbells than we've been led to believe. If Lamar Gant can deadlift over

700 pounds with severe scoliosis and 15-year-old girls can squat 300 pounds with form that would make an actual strength coach turn away in shame and embarrassment, bad form cannot be all that dangerous, at least in terms of the potential for catastrophic injury. Weightlifting, powerlifting, and weight training are actually far safer activities than, say, soccer, despite the fact that most people do lots of things wrong most of the time. The vast majority of the serious injuries and fatalities associated with weight training are the result of unspotted bench pressing, usually at home. The chances of needing to leave the gym in an ambulance are vanishingly small (although once, a long time ago, a new guy actually called an ambulance when his legs began to cramp after a squat workout – I was gone at the time). During the thirty years I have been in the gym business, aside from a few broken toes, there have been no serious injuries at my gym that required medical attention.

Now, there have been lots of people who have gone to the doctor unnecessarily – me among them, long ago – for injuries that doctors are not particularly good at either understanding or treating. It may have seemed necessary at the time, because we are raised to think that you see a doctor when you're hurt. But after the third time you hear, "You just pulled a muscle. Take these pain killers, these muscle relaxers, and these anti-inflammatories. And quit lifting so much weight," you quit going to the doctor unless bright blood is actually spurting from an artery.

As a general rule, acute injuries in the gym are usually back tweaks, the kind of thing that chiropractors and PTs can sometimes help with. These injuries are most often spinal in nature, affecting the facet joints, one of the small ligaments between adjacent vertebrae, the nerves immediately proximal to these structures, or a combination of the three. Sometimes an intervertebral disc is involved, but not usually. When chiropractic or physical therapy works, it has been my experience that it usually does so within two or three visits, thirty not being particularly useful for anything except the bottom line of the chiropractor or PT. Pain killers and muscle relaxers don't help them heal faster, but they may make it easier to get to sleep and to train around and through the injury, which *will* help it heal faster (but which is usually advised against by the people who write the prescriptions). Anti-inflammatories are quite useful but do not require a prescription; I buy my Equate ibuprofen at Wal-Mart.

Back tweaks usually occur in one of two situations: 1) under light weights where good form is not being observed, either through negligence or inexperience, or 2) under heavy weights, where good form breaks down due to the load. They are almost never "muscle tears," because muscle tears usually occur in muscle bellies, in muscles that either accelerate or decelerate motion around a joint that moves at a high angular velocity, like a quad, a hamstring, or a rotator cuff muscle. Massage may help the muscles relax, but massage in and of itself cannot affect the cause of the pain. These types of injuries usually heal within two weeks whether you do anything to treat them or not, unless a disc injury has occurred. Competitive lifters get used to them and learn to train around them, often by performing the very exercise that caused the injury using perfect form, very light weights, and very high reps.

Good Form

It is not impossible to pull other muscles, and hamstring, quad, and pec tears occur even when using good form. Tears happen when the force of the muscle contraction is overcome by the resistance so rapidly that it cannot be compensated for by the other muscles. Leg muscles tear when running or when training with weight explosively; pecs tear when benching explosively, or with max weights that, once the tear starts, cannot be unloaded quickly enough. Sometimes tears result from agonist/antagonist strength imbalances, or fatigue, or when the extensibility of muscle bellies is exceeded by uncontrolled range of motion. Sometimes it is bad form.

Overuse injuries, another common variety, usually involve joints or the muscular tissue in very close proximity to joints. Bad form often predisposes one to these types of injuries, by causing joints to move in ways that tendons and ligaments are not happy with. Many chronic shoulder injuries started out in life as incorrect bench presses and grew up to be rotator cuff surgeries. The mechanism of this rotten situation will become apparent.

The reality of the situation is that when a lifter reaches the point where the amount of weight lifted becomes more important than increasing strength – when you lift as a sport, not to strengthen for another sport or for general fitness – you will be lifting enough weight to get hurt. Any competitive sport is dangerous; lifting as a sport itself is competitive; and that's just the way things are. Lifting for strength and conditioning is different, and much, *much* safer.

Strong Enough?

Bad form is to be deplored not just for its potential risk but also for its potential to keep us from getting stronger. This is because bad form occurs when a movement pattern is executed inefficiently, the bar being moved by bones traveling through space in a way that does not maximize musculoskeletal efficiency. And this occurs when work is being avoided by muscles that should be doing it, in favor of muscles that shouldn't. It happens when novice lifters learn things wrong, something that may not be entirely their fault. It also happens when experienced lifters allow their form to deteriorate, either unconsciously, through a lack of concern for good form, or intentionally, by cheating a movement to lift more weight than their strength using good form will permit.

This biomechanical stuff is rather dry, and that's probably why sensible, interesting people don't either write it, read about it, or call in about it on Art Bell. So I'll try to make it this as "interesting" as I can.

For example, when you allow your hips to come up before your chest in a deadlift – when your back angle changes before the bar leaves the floor – your knees have extended. You know this because your back angle can't change unless either your knee or your hip angle changes, and in this case it's primarily your knee angle. This means that the muscles that extend your knees, your quads, did in fact extend your knees but did not lift the bar when they did so. They moved the knee joints, pulling the shins away from the bar, but did not produce any work against the load. Now when the bar is lifted, the entire work of the deadlift will be done without significant contribution from the quadriceps.

This means that the hip extensors – the glutes and hamstrings – have to do all the work by themselves. The normal job the hip extensors do as the bar comes off the floor is essentially isometric; they maintain the back angle by anchoring the pelvis, so that the quads can extend the knees to push the bar away from the floor. It's not that the glutes and hamstrings aren't working at the bottom of the pull – they certainly are – but their work at this position enables the quads to do their job. So if you fail to keep your chest up as the bar leaves the floor, you allow the quads to puss out, changing the role of the hamstrings from antagonists to agonists off the floor. This should be obvious to even the dullest Sasquatch, or "Bigfoot", if you prefer the colloquial term.

This is bad form and a perfect example of its effects. Bad form changes the nature of an exercise from efficient to inefficient; it changes the way the bones move the load, and in doing so changes the contribution of the muscles that are supposed to move the bones. Instead of all the muscles in the system making their anatomically efficient contribution to the loaded movement, when form is bad some muscles do more than they are supposed to and some do less. You know this because a stiff-legged deadlift (SLDL), the intentional version of this particular example of bad form, has a lower 1RM than a deadlift even though the bar moves the same distance. A SLDL is a useful assistance exercise when done as an adjunct to deadlift training, but when it comes time to lift the most weight, it would be terribly unproductive to confuse the two movements. Aside from the reduced efficiency, the SLDL's back angle places maximal torque on the low back, by increasing the length of the lever arm between the load and the axis of rotation (i.e., the extending hip joint) and by applying that load at right angles to the moment arm. This dramatically increases the stress on the muscles and ligaments responsible for maintaining spinal extension – not a bad thing if you're doing it intentionally (SLDL), but counterproductive if you're trying for a new PR (no new PR), as even the most inexperienced time traveler will tell you.

Why would a lifter find it advantageous to intentionally or deliberately avoid using a major group of muscles that obviously make an important contribution to a lift? After all, if the hamstrings and glutes are strong enough to do all the work of lifting the bar off the floor without the help of the quads, they are certainly strong enough to function in their proper isometric role of anchoring the back angle so the quads can work. Well, it's seldom intentional, because if it is, it's a SLDL. And it's never an advantage to move a load inefficiently. It is usually just learned wrong through a lack of feedback at a crucial time in the learning process. Or sometimes it's form creep, bad technique acquired so gradually that it is never perceived as wrong until someone else does you the favor of pointing it out (and let's hope that you're gracious about it when it happens). Sometimes it is the result of a movement pattern altered when training through an injury, and the resulting strength imbalance may fail to be addressed when the injury is finally healed. But failure to correct it once you know about the problem is either laziness or an unwillingness to back off to lighter weights until good form has time to strengthen the muscles that have not been making their proper contribution. This was identified as a problem by CIA remote viewers back in the 1970's.

Furthermore, I'll go out on what I hope is not too skinny a limb here and state that bad form in all basic barbell exercise is of the same type: using muscles in ways that reduce efficiency, increase the chance of injury, and reduce training productivity by moving bones in ways that are not mechanically optimum. "Mechanically optimum" means keeping the load directly over the point of balance at the end of the kinetic chain (the mid-foot in standing barbell exercises and directly above the point on the bench where the vertical arms support the bar in the bench press) while moving the load with the shortest possible lever arms.

The concept of the lever arm, or moment arm, is important to understand. A lever arm is the distance along which force is applied to an axis of rotation, as with a wrench turning a bolt, or potential rotation, like the bar on your back applying force to your hips in a squat. The bones of the skeleton transfer force generated by the contraction of the muscles attached to them to the load, and the bones rotate at the joints. The part of the body between the load and the ground is referred to as the "kinetic chain" because it is what produces the movement. For all the barbell exercises that involve standing with or under the bar and that involve more than one joint in the movement, the greatest efficiency occurs when the weight is moved in a way that keeps it directly over the point on the ground where the weight of the system is in balance. For humans this point is the middle of the foot, because that is where the average weight distribution against the ground is centered. When the weight is heavy, all the movement of the weight must occur as nearly vertical to this point as possible, or the weight/body system is out of balance. The bones that transfer muscular force to the load must move in ways that keep the load over this position. Any skeletal position assumed during the movement that places the load over some point other than the mid-foot creates a lever arm between the load and the mid-foot, and that leverage adds to the resistance of the load. During the movement, if a lever arm is created between the mid-foot and the load, the effort being generated to move the load will change to an effort not to fall over on your ass. The only place this cannot happen is Area 51.

And even if the system is in balance over the foot, a lever arm may appear between the bar and the joints moving the bar. The distance between the joints extending under the load and the bar itself should be minimal, and if the length of the lever arm begins to exceed that which can be dealt with efficiently (as when you lean back away from a press), the lift will not be completed. This is the principle that enables alien craft to travel between star systems to kidnap unsuspecting victims for bizarre rituals that are only remembered under hypnosis.

Squatting and pulling from the ground both involve the generation of force by the hips and legs as they react against the ground, and the transfer of that force up the rigid spine to the load, which is either at the top of the spine in the case of the squat or hanging from it at the end of the arms in a pull. Squats and pulls differ in 1) the position of the bar at the point of force transfer (on the back or hanging from the arms), 2) the hip/knee range of motion dictated by the location of the bar (on the back versus on the ground), 3) the eccentric versus concentric nature of the two movements,

and 4) the amount of Nazi mind-control technology
involved.

For any squat, short lever arms are a part of the
balance problem, because the squat carries the bar on the
torso (or directly above it in the case of the overhead squat),
with a roughly equal distribution of body mass on either side
of the bar, so that the center of mass of the system is
essentially directly over the mid-foot. If the thighs and feet
are parallel and the rigid back is at the right angle to keep the
bar over the mid-foot, the hips can very efficiently solve the
problem of maintaining balance and short, efficient lever
arms. The common form problems in the squat upset this
balanced lever arm relationship and result in the
biomechanical inefficiencies that typify bad form. If the
knees cave in toward the middle, the quads are being asked to
do the job of the adductors, and, as in our earlier example of
the hamstrings in the deadlift, they are strong enough to do
it, even though it leaves the adductors untrained and
ultimately weakens maximal squat capacity. The femur and
the tibia, which normally operate vertically parallel as the
knee flexes and extends, deviate inward (toward the midline)
at the knee, squishing the lateral meniscus in the knee joint
due to the uneven load. The bones move wrong, the muscles
move them that way, and the muscles get trained wrong as a
result. And this is how you know that the Extraterrestrials
are responsible for the recent increase in gas prices.

The problems are obvious if the back rounds in either
a squat or a deadlift. It is hard to maintain a tight isometric
spinal erector contraction with a heavy bar hanging from
your shoulders. If your back is weak because you let it get

that way, the trunk muscles fail to do their job and thus remain unworked in favor of letting the spinal ligaments try to keep the vertebrae in position. Since they can't do this very well, the intervertebral relationships go bad, with the discs and the facet joints jammed into positions they'd rather not occupy. And since the muscles fail to maintain a rigid trunk, the force being transmitted from the legs and hips through the trunk to the load – whether sitting on the upper back or the shoulders, supported overhead, or hanging from the arms – gets partially absorbed in the wiggle. This makes for a sloppy job of applying the force, like hitting a burglar with a pillow instead of a bat. And it's all because you failed to maintain the correct spinal alignment, either when you were learning or when the weight got heavy later. But then again it could have something to do with Air Force con trails.

The deadlift is different from the squat in that most of the body is behind the bar, not under it, as it hangs from the arms under the shoulders. Think about the difference between a barbell deadlift and a trap-bar "deadlift" and you can see the situation. The load, which consists of you and the bar, still needs to be over the middle of the foot, and as the weight gets heavier the position of the center of mass of the bar/body system more closely approximates the position of the bar (as your mass relative to that of the bar becomes increasingly less significant). Short lever arms for the deadlift are maintained by keeping the shoulder blades over the bar, with the best back angle your anthropometry will permit. This is a means of keeping the linear distance between the hip and the scapula as short as possible – as vertical a back as the proper bar/scapula relationship will permit – so that the lever arm formed by the back is as short as possible. Likewise, the bar has to stay over the mid-foot so that the lever arm between the bar and the balance point on the floor is as short as possible, preferably zero. This is also true for cleans and snatches as they leave the floor, up to the point where the second pull starts. And just what were those lights in the sky last night? C'mon, be honest with us *this one time.*

In overhead pressing, the muscles that attach to the humerus and the elbow must drive them up while the bar held in the hands at the end of the forearms stays in position directly above the elbows and directly over the mid-foot. It involves a simultaneous elbow flexion and shoulder extension, while the torso is held in the position that maximizes the efficiency of the actions of the shoulder and elbow joints against the load. For the press, if the bar stays in balance over the mid-foot as it should, the primary lever arm in question is the horizontal distance between the bar and the shoulder joint. This is shortest when the bar is closest to the shoulder, and consequently the face, which makes the nose a wonderful target for the bar for efficient pressing. The most common form problem involves the failure to maintain this close distance, whether through pushing the bar away, leaning back away from the bar, or failing to get under it as it passes the top of the head. In all three of these cases, the trunk muscles fail to hold the torso in the correct position close to the bar, placing the pressing muscles themselves in the unwelcome position of having to overcome what might be rapidly increasing leverage problems. The role of the abs in pressing is important, and good pressers have thick abs. Bad pressers don't develop thick abs because they are too busy leaning back, not using them. And in all likelihood, bad pressers are responsible for the recent rash of animal mutilations we've been hearing so much about.

Failing to maintain a vertical forearm creates another lever arm, one that should not even be there, between the bar and the elbow. This relationship normally involves no torque at all. But if the anterior chest muscles – the pecs and frontal deltoids – fail to keep the humerus pulled forward so that the elbow stays under the bar and the forearm stays vertical, the smaller forearm muscles are called upon to overcome the torque produced when the bar is in front of the elbow. If the elbows, conversely, are lifted up too high, like the rack position of the clean, another lever arm is created that should not be there; the remaining movement will look more like a triceps extension than a press. This happens when the lats fail to do their job of providing posterior antagonist support for the humerus as the delts and triceps act on the load that should be right over the elbow, a problem compounded when the torso fails to remain upright and rigid. The Reptilians, of course, solved this problem eons ago while building the Pyramids.

Bench pressing is simpler because the kinetic chain – the distance between the hands and the upper back where it mashes into the bench – is shorter and therefore involves fewer joints. Like the press, benching involves a shoulder flexion and an elbow extension, and like the press it depends on a tight lineup between the bar, the elbow, and the shoulder joint to minimize the length of the lever arm between the load and the shoulder. We are not powerlifters, most of us anyway, and we use the bench to get strong, not really to see how much we can bench. So we need to use the technique that most effectively strengthens the muscles used in the bench press. Heaving the bar up using the hips as a part of the rebound is an excellent way of lifting more weight, since it recruits lower body muscles into the exercise. It is also an excellent way of avoiding an opportunity to strengthen the upper-body muscles that the bench is supposed to work. Had the Atlanteans only known this, they might still be around today. Or maybe they are.

A missed bench press most commonly involves the elbows failing to remain directly beneath the bar when the delts and the pecs fail to do their job of keeping the bar and the joints lined up. The elbow typically drops down toward the ribcage, increasing the horizontal distance between the bar and the shoulder. This is normally accompanied by bridging the hips up off the bench, which, among other things, attempts to shorten this lever arm by increasing the angle of the chest and bringing the elbows more in line with the shoulders. This is a little hard to visualize, but no harder than imagining the problems involved in the enormous task of constructing the Face on Mars.

There are countless other examples of bad form, and if you think in these terms as you train and watch others train, it will become apparent that what is happening is the incorrect use of your skeleton, which results in the incorrect use of your muscles. Good form is not arbitrary, and its purpose is not aesthetics. It is based on a logical analysis of the relevant mechanics – what works and what doesn't – and what you or I feel about that should be irrelevant. Good form is based on human anatomy and the physics of movement, and should be harder science than that which is normally discussed late at night on the radio. It may not be as much fun, but it will be of more immediate benefit than Edgar Cayce could ever have predicted.

Good Form

Strong Enough?

"By 1975 some experts feel that food shortages will have escalated the present level of world hunger and starvation into famines of unbelievable proportions. Other experts, more optimistic, think the ultimate food-population collision will not occur until the decade of the 1980s."

Paul Ehrlich
Ramparts Earth Day issue (1970)

"Let's figure that out again--1948.5 plus 51.4 equals 1999.9--around September of the year 1999. Now, we are not date-setters! Of that day and hour knoweth no man, no, not he angels of heaven, but my father only (Matthew 24:36). But wait! Don't say, 'No one can know the APPROXIMATE time when Christ will return,' for Jesus also said in verse 33 that we will know when it is near, even at the doors."

Jack Van Impe
Perhaps Today magazine (1993)

Be Alive. Be *Very* Alive.

Speaking of talk radio, Mike McConnell, the best talk show host currently on the air anywhere in the country – and by extension, the world – has suggested that the single most important contributing factor in the "obesity epidemic" is the relatively recent introduction of air conditioning and heating. This makes a huge amount of sense, given the fact that most of the time we are inside we are sitting on our asses and that air conditioning encourages us to stay inside. Heating used to be accomplished in a more manual fashion, predicated on hauling something inside to burn. People in more northerly climates enjoy a more friendly outdoor experience in the summer, and those of us cursed with a Texas address in the summer get compensated with comparatively mild winters. But the net effect of air conditioning technology is an increased average amount of time spent indoors sitting on our asses.

This leads to problems, because we have not spent the last 65 million or so years finely honing our physiology to watch *Oprah*. Like it or not, we are the product of a very long process of adaptation to a harsh physical existence, and the past couple of centuries of comparative ease and plenty has not had time to change our genome. We humans are at our best when our existence mirrors, or at least simulates, the one we are still genetically adapted to live. And that is the purpose of exercise. But the problems that are created by ignoring this are not just physical; diabetes, obesity, osteoporosis, heart disease, hypertension, sarcopenia, and bad breath are only a part of what's wrong with the way the 21st century treats its precious children.

To a very great extent, the health problems experienced by the members of the ridiculous culture in which we live are self-inflicted. They are result of the reluctance of the bulk of the population to do anything that is either physically hard or something that they don't want to do. People seem to have acquired the idea that they have the inalienable right to stroll through life without either having sweated, picked up anything heavy, worked hard, or eaten less than they wanted at every meal. This approach is, of course, wrong. And it has resulted in a lot of expensive, unattractive, and entirely preventable problems amongst people who seem puzzled about why things aren't going well.

We have become lazy. I know you've heard this before, and I know it doesn't necessarily apply to you or me in the same way it does to the general public. But I dare you to read Steven Pressfield's *Gates of Fire*, his marvelous retelling of the Spartan's battle with the Persians at Thermopylae, and tell me that you're not a pussy.

It hasn't been that long – just a couple of generations – since life was more physical than it is now. My dad was born in 1920, and his father quite literally walked from Tennessee to Texas when he was ten years old. And probably thought nothing of it. You and I, godlike specimens that we are, would never be faced with a comparable task because it has been made unnecessary under the normal circumstances of modern existence. We might decide to do something silly like ride our bikes that far for fun, but a mandatory task of that magnitude would never occur in the modern First World.

And this is good, because lots of people died on that trip and the others like it that were made necessary by the transportation technology of the day. Unnecessary death is never good. But it is also bad in that the ability to rise to such an occasion has been essentially lost.

McConnell hates the term "wellness" as much as I do. Wellness is what we say when we mean Ineffective Exercise and USDA Dietary Guidelines, both of which are designed to be easy to do and to pay lip service to a concept that most people know is good and right but don't have the nads to actually follow. Wellness means having a salad and a baked potato after your aerobics class. It means enjoying increased longevity: getting to watch more episodes of *Oprah*! It means making an attempt at doing something harder than sitting at your desk, and that the attempt itself is good enough. Mainly it means that just being "well" is good enough. Well, "well" is not good enough, and we need to quit acting like it is.

Granted, modern western society could benefit immeasurably from a large-scale movement in the direction of even this watered-down version of optimal human existence. But, the general public being what it is, the tide that floats all the boats is going to have to be a pretty damn big tide, and "wellness" just hasn't got that much water. Those of us that actually train should understand why it's good: that physically – and by extension, mentally – difficult tasks are normal and natural to our existence, that they have been since the inception, and that this is the reason they make us healthier. Overcoming the challenges presented by these tasks makes us generally better as humans, and if the task does not rise to the level of a challenge it fails to provide this benefit. It may make you "well", but it won't make you anything more. Maintaining our own high training standards will have the long term effect of raising those of the general public as well, for which favor they will all owe us a beer.

Hard training does all these fabulous things because physical difficulties are always accompanied by the mental and emotional effects those difficulties create. Finishing a very heavy set of 20 squats is as much a mental task as it is a physical. The 17th rep is done under conditions of accumulating lactic acid, the inability to satisfy an increasingly severe oxygen debt, blurred vision, aching feet, and a sensation that must be vaguely akin to drowning. And then you have to decide whether to do the 18th, which isn't going to feel any better. The 19th and 20th are going to be worse, and most people who have not experienced this before will quit. The ones who don't will learn something about their own limits, and about the temporary nature of such adversity. Amazingly enough, the weight is not that heavy – the first rep and the last rep are both "light" compared to the way a heavy single feels – and the challenge is not the generation of enough force to get back up out of the bottom. The challenge is doing it when you feel like you are about to die, when things other than making the bar go up would logically seem more important. If you have never done a set of 20 with a weight that you previously thought was a 10-rep max, you should try it sometime.

Be Alive. Be Very Alive.

Max sets of 20 are nasty, sinister bastards, very hard to do for more than a few weeks at a time because of the mental aspects of the task. Quite literally, you have about 5 minutes to enjoy the fact that the set is over before the realization dawns that you have to do it again next week. I have often spent the day with an awful sense of dread for weeks at a time while I was doing them until, finally, progress on them slowed to a stop and I could honorably change squat workouts to something else. After this, pretty much everything else seemed easy, at least in the weight room. I learned later that there is significant carryover to things outside the weight room.

The two things that most influence our physical appearance, exercise and diet, share in common the fact that doing them correctly means choosing to do things that involve discomfort. It is unfortunately impossible to sit down to the table and eat all you want every time you eat. Jobs that make this possible – like being a galley slave or a field hand – are not terribly common since the invention of modern labor-saving devices like engines and tractors. Leaving the table before you're full involves you making a decision not to do something you'd rather do. Whether this rises to the level of actual discomfort depends on your personal relationship with your cheeseburger, but hunger is a powerful sensation for most people that don't suffer from an eating disorder. Try walking into a restaurant sometime and just watching other people eat when you're hungry yourself. Even younger guys trying to gain weight find that the requirements – eating *more* than you want to every time you eat – involve some degree of temporary discomfort.

Strong Enough?

Eating to obtain a positive result as opposed to mindlessly feeding yourself to satiety requires discipline, although not as much as the last three reps of the set of 20. And if you can't make yourself stay away from the fourth piece of chicken, you're never going to do the set of 20 anyway. Supper might be a good place to practice setting easy little goals for yourself that require some discipline to accomplish, so you can get in the habit of being in better control of your behavior.

The problem with this is that when we stop expecting things from ourselves, our expectations of other people go down as well. Here's an example of what happens when our expectations get significantly diminished. This unfortunate event recently transpired in England:

Seven schoolgirls have sparked a major search and rescue mission – after being frightened by a herd of cows. The terrified pupils, aged 14 and 15, were on a geography field trip in Swanage, Dorset, when they sent out an SOS. They were dropped off three miles from their outdoor centre and told to find their way back using a map. But the teenagers, from St Albans in Hertfordshire, got stuck on a hill when they came across a herd of cows in a field blocking their way.

A coastguard rescue team, police and an ambulance were scrambled to rescue them after one of the girls called for help on her mobile phone.

I say let the cows eat them. They are already useless, because they've been taught – at home and at their ridiculous school – that they can't do anything for themselves. I say had they been doing PR sets of 20 squats, a herd of English cows would not present so intimidating an obstacle. And at this late date squats may be their only chance at a life free from shame and embarrassment.

Now, I realize that there are hundreds of millions of individual examples of people throughout the US and Europe who have grown to a ripe old age without having engaged in either hard physical work or hard physical exercise. So why does it matter so much that people are out of shape, especially if it has no apparent effect on longevity? Well, I don't know about you, but I'm not interested in being 85 if I have to hire somebody to help me get up off of the toilet. Very often in discussions of the public health benefits of exercise, the only consideration is longevity; an 80 year-old man with Alzheimer's might argue that longevity is not always a benefit, if he could.

So let me say something a little meatier: you owe it to yourself and the millions of lives that generated yours to live as though you appreciated it. Over and above the fact that you're healthier – and as a result cost everybody less money and aggravation while you're here – there is just something wrong with getting up every day and moving through your existence with the least possible effort. Doing it this way makes you more than merely less than optimum. It makes you afraid of cows, and unable to understand that you should not be.

If your expectations are always those of someone content to live without physical challenge, then when it comes time for mental, moral, or emotional challenge you fail to meet it because you are out of practice. Meeting and overcoming obstacles are skills that can be honed, as opposed to talents with which we are born. The best way to prepare for the inevitable shit that life occasionally hands us all is to live in a way that prepares you for it. If you can treat personal tragedy like a heavy set of 20 squats, you'll do better than someone who has never met any challenge. Intentionally placing yourself in the position of having to complete a task when you don't know if you can is the single best way of preparing to be in that position unintentionally. And that, my friends, is the way your training should be approached, so that you get more out of it than just "wellness".

Be Alive. Be Very Alive.

"The problem with people who have no vices is that generally you can be pretty sure they're going to have some pretty annoying virtues."

Elizabeth Taylor

Strong Enough?

(Photograph courtesy of Tony Budding)

Strong Enough?

Strong Enough?

"Dave Rutabaugh is an ignorant scoundrel. I disapprove of his very existence. I considered ending it myself on several occasions but ... self-control got the better of me."

Dennis Quaid
as Doc Holiday in Wyatt Earp

"Now, I don't want to kill you, and you don't want to be dead."

Danny Glover
as Malachi Johnson in Silverado

Strong Enough?